CONTEMPORARY COMMUNITY HEALTH SERIES

CONTEMPORARY ATTITUDES TOWARD MENTAL ILLNESS

CONTEMPORARY ATTITUDES

Guido M. Crocetti
Herzl R. Spiro
Iradj Siassi

TOWARD MENTAL ILLNESS

University of Pittsburgh Press

Publication of this book was made possible by a grant from the Maurice Falk Medical Fund. The Fund, however, is not the author, publisher, or proprietor of the material presented here and is not to be understood, by virtue of its grant, as endorsing any statement made or expressed herein.

Library of Congress Cataloging in Publication Data

Crocetti, Guido M. (birth date)
Contemporary attitudes toward mental illness.

(Contemporary community health series)
Bibliography: p. 229
1. Mental illness—Public opinion. I. Spiro, Herzl R., (birth date) joint author. II. Siassi, Iradj, (birth date) joint author. III. Title. IV. Series.
RC454.4.C76 301.15'43'61689 73-80071
ISBN 0-8229-3273-3

Feffer and Simons, Inc., London
Manufactured in the United States of America

Publication of this book was made possible
by a grant from the Maurice Falk Medical Fund.

Contents

Introduction: The Issue

Illness constitutes a universal phenomenon. Every rational man is cognizant of the possibility that illness may, at any moment, strike him or those he holds dear. This awareness plays perhaps the most significant role in the universal compassion for the sick, the privileges attached to the sick role, and the tolerance for the deviant behavior of the ill person.

For the social animal—man—mental illness is no less universal than physical illness. Throughout his life-span, every man is subject to psychological and social forces that at times may overwhelm him. Should this awareness of personal vulnerability not evoke similar feelings toward the mentally ill? The religious and philosophic mind-body dichotomy, which granted the mind a favorable and privileged position, is seen by some as the possible source of a special fear of mental illness—a fear of impairment of the more valued possession.

Whether we view illness from a sociological or a psychological viewpoint, the problems confronting the physically ill and the mentally ill should be parallel. The suspension of normal behavior is typical in both groups of illness, as are the need for special attention, an unusual dependence on others, and, in modern times, the possibility of confinement in a hospital.

How does the public view the mentally sick person in comparison with the physically sick person? Some researchers suggest the two views are radically different. For example, for many years, certain sociologists have placed ethnic outgroups, deviants, and the mentally ill in one classification. For others, this dubious method of classification by convenience has no foundation. To silence doubts, one would need to know what the public thinks of the mentally sick person and, further, what the basic distinctions are between mental diseases and all other diseases—distinctions that would foster such mutually incompatible points of view.

This book is a study of American society's attitudes toward its mentally ill members. The study is based on a detailed review of public-attitude investigations of the past two decades and three recent research projects in Baltimore, Maryland. Although the field of research into public attitudes toward the mentally ill is relatively new, researchers have already become polarized into two factions: those who see society as rejecting the mentally ill, displaying hostility toward them, and closing its ranks against them; and those who believe that society is generally accepting of the mentally ill, is compassionate toward them, and is willing to accept them into its ranks. The first group sees the public as unable or unwilling to identify mental illness as illness, as pessimistic about the outcome of treatment of the mentally ill, and as disinclined to think about mental illness. The second group sees the average American as having enough mental health information to know about mental illness, to see mental illness as illness, and to be optimistic about the outcome of its treatment. The first group sees an all-encompassing stigma attached to the mentally ill; the second group does not. Granted the reductionism implicit in suggesting this dichotomy into two factions, it is still the case that fundamental differences of opinion exist. These factions may not be united in themselves; nonetheless, they express essentially different concepts of society's attitudes.

The idea for this book came about through reflection on the contrast between the above-mentioned views. A dichotomy of another kind was also subject for reflection: the present dialectical tension between the majority of mental health professionals who consider mental illness to be an illness requiring clinical help and a small number of mental health professionals and a growing number of sociologists who would like to view mental illness as a form of social deviance rather than as an illness.

The complex and universal problem of mental illness has an imperative need for contributions from many divergent disciplines. Yet, by and large, both the scientific progress so sorely dependent on cooperation between these disciplines and the rational application of scientific data have been hampered by excessive factionalism, controversy, and dissension.

In spite of the need for dispassionate discourse, the debate has frequently degenerated into passionate polemics. In spite of the obvious need for cooperative and painstaking research, there has often been intolerance with other researchers' premises and perspectives. Although it is irrefutable that impatience with the status quo may provide the spur for movement and progress, equally irrefutable is the prospect of diminishing returns: that impatience may become destructive and self-defeating. For example, it is both irrational and unscientific to ignore or denigrate the enormous contributions of psychoanalytic research to the understanding of mental illness, as some are doing with the rationale that psychoanalytic theory has not solved all the riddles of mental illness. It would be equally regrettable not to welcome the valuable contributions from other disciplines, notably sociology. The growing awareness of the social aspects of mental illness in the last two decades has brought much-needed contributions from socially oriented psychiatrists, psychologists, sociologists, cultural anthropologists, and others.

Over-sociologization of mental illness, however, gives rise to serious questions. The reduction or expansion of mental illness into the framework of "deviant behavior" needs careful examination. The increasing community involvement in decision-making in the mental health field, the stipulation that there should be maximum feasible participation by the community for the granting of federal funds for community mental health centers, and, in a few cases, the growing community control over mental health services make the assessment of public attitudes toward the mentally ill critical and urgent.

If, in fact, the public does have hostile and punitive attitudes toward the mentally ill, reasonable application of available knowledge should improve these attitudes, which unaltered would impede the development of community-based services. However, before some of the scarce resources of mental health programs are diverted to such efforts, there should be some soul-searching. What documentation can be found of the prevalence of such attitudes?

Many months of discussion among ourselves and our colleagues and friends preceded the actual writing of this book. The emergence of an overall scheme was a gradual process; in fact, both the acceptance and the rejection viewpoints were represented in our thinking as the research began. It was the review of the available sources in the research field, and the examination of our findings in the light of others, that served to crystallize our thinking.

A brief, critical evaluation seemed necessary to discover how researchers have come to mutually incompatible conclusions and why these mutually incompatible views are held by two groups of professionals. The best approach seemed first to review the developments in this field of research during the last two decades and then to examine these studies in the light of the detailed findings of three studies carried out in Baltimore over the past ten years.

There is a natural division of the work into several chapters. In chapter 1, an effort is made to comb the available literature, to select findings from a large number of sources, and to examine the plausibility of various hypotheses in the light of the accumulated data from different studies. The aim in this effort is fourfold: to provide a history of mental health research, to induce mental health professionals to reexamine their views in the light of the latest findings, to understand how some of the current beliefs were created and to shed some light on the sources which contributed to their creation, and finally to create for students interested in this field the opportunity to embark on a course of independent reading and study, unfettered by the undue influence of a chance encounter. In chapter 2, the concepts of stereotyping, stigma, and prejudice are examined with particular relevance to mental illness. The theoretical relationship between prejudicial, stigmatizing attitude formation and the sick role potentially accorded the mentally ill is considered. At the end of these two chapters, a "theory of rejection" is explicated. Five testable corollaries to this hypothesis are described.

Chapters 3 through 9 contain specific study methods and the results of the systematic examination of the "theory of rejection." Chapter 10 and the conclusion discuss these experimental findings.

Throughout the book, it is our hope to summarize fairly, to provide sufficient description so that others may replicate our studies, and to differentiate conclusions built on data from those based on speculation; in short to move away from the acrimony of opposing groups toward scientific inquiry (inasmuch as that is possible in a difficult field like social psychiatry). Although this volume may often fall short of that goal, we hope that its intent may have more influence than its shortcomings on subsequent reports.

PART I

A Review of the Literature

CHAPTER 1

Empirical Issues

"The mentally ill have always been with us—to be feared, marvelled at, laughed at, pitied, or tortured, but all too seldom cured." Thus the first sentence of a well-known history of psychiatry illustrates the wide range of responses to the mentally ill (Alexander and Selesnick 1966). Historians and students of primitive medicine such as Sigerist (1951) or Ackerknecht (1942a, 1942b) also find that the mentally ill are treated in many different ways.

The conflicting viewpoints of the nature of mental illness can be traced to the dawn of recorded history. Are the symptoms a sign of closeness to the gods, of possession by evil spirits, or of disease to be alleviated by trephining and herbs? To Albertus Magnus and his famous student Thomas Aquinas, psychotic symptoms meant an inability to chose between right and wrong and thus an immunity from moral condemnation.

Ellenberger (1970), looking at the great cultural movements of Western civilization from the end of the Middle Ages to the nineteenth century, speaks of the Renaissance as a period of "great interest in mental illness" and "in the multiform manifestations ascribed to that peculiar faculty of the mind, *imaginatio*. The study of imagination, one of the legacies of the Renaissance to the following centuries, was to become the main source of early dynamic psychiatry" (p. 194). The succeeding period, the Baroque, was a period of "witchhunting and belief in devilish possession" (p. 195). The third cultural movement, the Enlightenment, influenced religious circles by dispelling belief in the devil and hence lead to the end of witch trials. The Enlightenment "influenced psychiatry in many ways, beginning with its laicization. Many symptoms, which had been considered to be the effects of witchcraft or possession, came to be considered as forms of mental illness. Efforts were being made to understand mental illness in a scientific manner" (p. 197). The fourth cultural movement, Romanticism, fostered a preoccupation with the nature of mental illness, with mental hygiene, and with the concept of creative illness. "The Romantics' interest in mental illness was furthered by the fact that in that period, numerous mental institutions were opened and began to be headed by specialized physicians who lived constantly with their patients" (p. 210). The Romantic period was supplanted in the middle of the nineteenth century by Positivism, "the cultural trend that forwarded organicist psychiatry and prevailed throughout the second half of the nineteenth century" (p. 887).

This historical diversity of attitudes toward the mentally ill may help to put into perspective modern North American research on the subject. The systematic study of the public's information about and attitudes toward mental illness and the mentally ill is a fairly new phenomenon, yet the reports of different investigations have sometimes seemed to be as divergent as if they spanned two millennia rather than two decades. This chapter will attempt to identify clearly the most important differences in these attitudinal studies by carefully and critically reviewing the literature. Examining these differences will permit the formulation of testable hypotheses about current public attitudes toward the mentally ill.

Public Attitudes Toward the Mentally Ill

The majority of the findings examined here are surveys which attempt to define attitudes toward the mentally ill by measuring the public's knowledge of various aspects of mental illness, responses to statements about mental illness and the mentally ill, and desire to maintain social distance between itself and the mentally ill. Naturally, the distance that an individual wishes to keep between himself and the members of any identifiable group cannot be measured by one simple response. Working with someone or living in his neighborhood does not entail the same degree of intimacy as rooming with or marrying him. Therefore, different people will allow or disallow different types of relationships according to the social distance they desire or feel. (Social distance is treated more fully in chapter 6.) It is sufficient to note here that the concept is basically sociological and does not consider the essentially psychological aspects of the relationships.

Although the idea of social distance as such was first used by Bogardus (1925), all of the early efforts in this field and much of the later work concern the social response to ethnic groups. The first application of the concept of social distance to attitudes toward the mentally ill was in 1943 when it was found that fear, stigmatization, and rejection characterized public feeling about the mentally ill (Allen 1943). After World War II, however, Ramsey and Siepp concluded that the public was moving toward a humanitarian and scientific view of the mentally ill (1948). Similarly, Woodward's Louisville, Kentucky, study found the growing public belief that "mental illness is a sickness and should evoke sympathetic understanding and . . . requires some form of professional treatment" (1951, p. 454).

The most influential of the early studies is the 1950 national survey conducted by Star at the National Opinion Research Center of the University of Chicago. Although Star never published a complete report of her results, she did give talks on her findings to the National Association for Mental Health in 1955 and to the Association for the Advancement of Public Opinion Research in 1957. She has also kindly supplied us with copies of the questionnaire and of an unpublished paper based on her results.

The study, originally called "The Dilemma of Mental

Illness," was based on a survey consisting of interviews with 3,500 individuals in a national-quota sample. One of the key parts of the interview included six case descriptions of mentally ill people: Frank Jones, a paranoid schizophrenic; Betty Smith, a simple schizophrenic; George Brown, a chronic anxiety neurotic; Mary White, a compulsive phobic; Bill Williams, an alcoholic; and Bobby Grey, a twelve-year-old child with a behavior disorder. Since these vignettes have been used in many subsequent studies, their complete descriptions are given in chapter 3.

After being presented with each case, the respondents were asked a series of questions: Did they think anything was wrong with the person described? What was wrong? Was it mental illness? Was it serious? Star found that only the paranoid schizophrenic was recognized as ill by a majority of the sample. She inferred from this that the public included only extreme psychosis accompanied by threatening, assaultive behavior in its actual working definition of mental illness.

Another group of Star's questions explored the respondent's knowledge about and opinion of special facilities for the treatment of the mentally ill. She concluded from the answers that although people were aware of such facilities, they were reluctant to think about them and were pessimistic about the treatment they provided.

June Bingham, representing the public in a round table discussion at the American Psychiatric Association meeting in 1950, expressed the idea that the public's concept of psychiatry came from its view of psychiatrists (Bingham 1951). She argued that the public derived its knowledge from lay literature such as novels, detective stories, plays, movies, and radio programs, rather than from the psychiatric literature. She stated that the layman's picture of a psychiatrist is that of a "cold-blooded machine, a devil, or a god" (1951, p. 601).

Another very influential study was conducted in 1951 by Elaine and John Cumming and reported in their book *Closed Ranks* (1957). This survey was carried out as a field experiment in mental health education in two small towns in Prairie County, Canada. One town, Blackfoot, population 1,500, was subjected to an intensive educational campaign, while the other town, Deerville, with 1,100 inhabitants, served as a control and had no campaign. Attitudes in both towns were surveyed with the same questionnaire form before and after the educational program. Using a Guttman scaling technique, the Cummings obtained two dimensions: social distance from the mentally ill and social responsibility for the mentally ill.

The preselected sample in Blackfoot consisted of the entire adult population. Unfortunately, the response rate to both of the Blackfoot surveys was low. Only 60 percent of the adult population responded before the educational campaign and the rate fell to 50 percent afterward. There are no data about the characteristics of the sample population who did not respond to either one or both of the questionnaires. In Deerville, the control community, no effort was made to achieve complete coverage. Responses were obtained from a sample of only 100 adults.

Of those who did respond, most were not reluctant to live in the same neighborhood with former mental patients, but they did not want to room with such people or to have any other close association with them. The educational campaign did not bring about any change in these attitudes. In response to the Star case descriptions, only the paranoid schizophrenic was considered mentally ill by a majority (69 percent) and only 45 percent of these considered the illness serious. The portion of the respondents who believed that the other vignettes described a mentally ill person ranged from 36 percent in the case of the simple schizophrenic to 4 percent for the compulsive phobic and the delinquent boy.

The Cummings concluded that the public's attitude was one of "denial, isolation, and insulation of mental illness" (1957, p. 119). They thought that this attitude explained the community's rejection of former mental patients and its tolerance of poor hospital conditions and patient isolation. They further theorized that this attitudinal social distance was necessary for "the reaffirmation of the solidarity of the social system in which the norms are not violated" (1957, p. 127) and that the isolation of the mentally ill reduced the guilt of those whose close friends or relatives had been sent to the state hospitals.

A somewhat different approach was used by Nunnally in his five-year study which started in 1954 at the Institute of Communication Research of the University of Illinois (Nunnally 1961). After applying the semantic differential to a nonrepresentative sample, he reached conclusions similar to those of Star and the Cummings: public attitudes were negative and the public was uninformed rather than misinformed about mental illness. One interesting part of Nunnally's research examines the role of the mass media in forming these public attitudes. In a systematic and large-scale content analysis of television, radio, newspapers, and magazines during a one-week period in 1955, he found that the mental patient was strongly stereotyped as dangerous and unpredictable. This stereotyped image was sometimes presented as much as a hundred times more frequently than the medically correct one.

Another interesting result was that possession of accurate information about mental illness correlated positively with age and education while attitudes toward the mentally ill did not. Nunnally concluded that educated and uneducated, old and young had negative attitudes toward mental illness. Physicians, such as general practitioners, were no exception, and their attitudes were as negative as the general public's. Nunnally felt that this latter finding had important implications for referrals and the use of services and preventive measures. He went on to offer specific suggestions for programs to change negative attitudes to positive ones. These ideas were based on his analysis of the data obtained from a sample of psychiatrists and psychologists who showed general agreement when asked about public-information programs. He urged that pathological behavior be explained to the public in an entirely new language which would eliminate former connotations. Nunnally's work exerted great influence on subsequent programs. Scheff, for example, referred to his study when arguing that the negative stereotype of the mentally ill changes slowly or not at all and that the mass media are a part of the social forces that maintain the stereotype (1963).

Yarrow, Clausen, and Robbins conducted a series of intensive interviews with the wives of mental hospital patients (1955). Of the thirty-five wives asked to participate, thirty-three did so. The interviews began at the time of the husbands' hospital admission and continued until they had either been home again for six months or been in the hospital for a year. The authors reported that the wives had "one predominant expectation—that mental illness is regarded by others as a stigma" (p. 34). They estimated, however, that only one-third of the study group reacted to the mental illness of their husbands by limiting any of their social interactions.

Working at the Survey Research Center of the University of Michigan, Gurin, Veroff, and Feld reached rather different conclusions in their monograph for the Joint Commission of Mental Illness and Health (1960). They discovered greater public knowledge about mental health and the mentally ill and improved public attitudes toward the mentally ill. However, they stated that the public's emotional reactions had not yet completely caught up with its newfound knowledge.

Ridenour (1961) was also led by her studies to different conclusions from Nunnally, Star, and the Cummings. She reported that by the late 1950s much improvement had taken place in individual attitudes toward mental illness. Many positive concepts of mental health had been accepted, and people showed a willingness to admit that they were ill and to seek psychiatric help.

In 1959, Freeman and Simmons sought to measure the amount of stigma attached to the mentally ill by interviewing a group of relatives of former mental hospital patients (1961a).

They noted that, except for Yarrow and Clausen, "surprisingly, consideration of the influence of stigma in discussions of the impact of mental illness has not been accompanied by systematic investigation of the phenomenon. A search of the relevant literature indicates that the stigma is usually discussed in vague and general terms. In the limited research on the problem, feelings of stigma ordinarily have been inferred from the content of non-directed interviews with a few informants; neither structured scales nor standard probes have been used in previous studies" (p. 312).

The sample studied by Freeman and Simmons consisted of 702 relatives of all the patients who had been discharged from a particular mental hospital in the first six months of 1959 and who had stayed in the community for a period longer than thirty days. Ninety-two percent of the sample were interviewed. Five structured items were used to measure feelings of stigma with less than 10 percent of the respondents applying more than one to their situation. The investigators felt that "only a small proportion of the study group feels stigmatized by having a mental patient in the home" (p. 315).

Freeman and Simmons further examined the minority "with-stigma" group, reporting that the feeling of stigma "appears to be associated with the degree of bizarre behavior on the part of the patient, the social class identification of family members and their personality characteristics" (p. 320). They concluded: "Our results, as well as the research of the Clausen group, do suggest that stigma—defined as sensitivity to the reactions of community associates, accompanied by withdrawal and concealment—is characteristic of only a minority of families of mental patients" (p. 316).

In 1961, the Joint Commission on Mental Illness and Health published its final report, *Action for Mental Health*. The report did not present any new data on public attitudes toward the mentally ill, but was simply meant to be a summary of the available evidence. Unfortunately, either because of the timing of its publications or for other reasons, the commission virtually ignored the findings of Woodward, Ridenour, and Gurin, and was predominantly influenced by the work of Star, Nunnally, and the Cummings. It presented a picture of rejection and punitive social response to mental illness, claiming that the public lacked recognition of mental illness as illness and that it tended to reject both mental patients and those who treated them. The report further described a "pervasive defeatism" concerning the mentally ill (p. xix). The tone of these statements, especially the last, obscured the encouraging findings of Ramsey and Siepp, Woodward, Ridenour, Freeman and Simmons, and Gurin, and left a totally pessimistic impression unjustified by the reported data.

In 1962 and 1963, P. Lemkau and Crocetti of the School of Public Health and Hygiene, Johns Hopkins University, published the results of their 1959-1960 study. This study is one of those examined in detail in chapters 3 to 9. However, since there is a sharp contrast between their findings and those of Star, Nunnally, and the Cummings, it is appropriate to summarize the 1962 paper here.

The population surveyed was located in a lower socioeconomic section of Baltimore that was to benefit from a planned expansion of home-care programs for the mentally ill. The study was an attempt to predict the possible fate of such programs.

Specially trained interviewers were used to survey a randomly selected sample. With a response rate of 90 percent, a total of 1,738 people were surveyed. Most of the questions in this study were identical to those used in previous surveys, and three of the six Star case descriptions were included. The people in the sample were relatively poor and uneducated. Nevertheless, a majority of the respondents identified all three vignettes as indicative of mental illness, felt that the described person should see a physician, and favored treating the mentally ill in the community. These responses did not support the concepts of denial, rejection, and isolation of mentally ill persons.

The following year, M. Lemkau examined professional and public attitudes toward the mentally ill in Carroll County, Maryland (1962). Her systematic probability sample of 139 appeared to be even better informed about mental illness than the Baltimore population. Eighty percent of those interviewed disagreed with the idea that all mental patients are dangerous, while 79 percent disagreed with the locked-door system as the best way to handle mental hospital patients. Ninety-five percent were aware of the existence of many forms of mental illness, and an overwhelming majority, ranging from 76 percent to 98 percent, responded favorably to questions about the home care of mental patients.

In 1962, the attitudes of the population of Easton, another Maryland community, were surveyed by Meyer (1964). Those in his probability sample of 100 were also knowledgeable about mental illness and were generally accepting of the mentally ill. Seventy-eight percent did not feel that all mental patients were dangerous, and 88 percent did not think that locked doors were the best way to handle mental hospital patients. Ninety-four percent knew of the existence of different forms of mental illness, with 89 percent in favor of home care for mental patients where medically appropriate.

In his book, ***Stigma,*** Goffman divides stigmatized individuals into the discredited and the discreditable (1963). The former are known bearers of a stigma, but the stigma of the latter is neither known nor immediately apparent. Placing former mental patients in the discreditable category, Goffman describes the patient's situation: "It is not that he must face prejudice against himself, but rather that he must face unwitting acceptance of himself by individuals who are prejudiced against persons of the kind he can be revealed to be. Wherever he goes his behavior will falsely confirm for the other that they are in the company of what in effect they demand but may discover they haven't obtained, namely, a mentally untainted person like themselves. By intention or in effect the ex-mental patient conceals information about his real social identity, receiving and accepting treatment based on false suppositions concerning himself" (p. 42). Lumping the ethnic outgroups, the mentally ill, the aged, and many others together, he states that "stigmatized persons have enough of their situations in life in common to warrant classifying all these persons together" (p. 146).

The Cummings undertook two small studies to explore their idea that a former mental hospital patient must consider himself stigmatized and "if he does not do so, sanctions will be brought to bear upon him automatically because [his disregard of his own stigmatization] is a direct challenge to the value system of the observer" (1965, p. 136). They saw this stigma as a form of ego damage and suggested that "in general, social competence, and, in particular, predictability or reliability are lost" (p. 136).

In the first study, twenty-two consecutively discharged patients of a state mental hospital were interviewed eight months after their return to the community. Eighteen of the former patients were living with relatives, and one relative of each patient was also interviewed. Stigma was inferred if the respondent saw the hospitalization as a source of shame or discrimination while answering questions about the patient's readjustment. Nine of the patients, or 41 percent, were judged to feel stigma, with four expressing shame and five expecting discrimination. One of the nine was a sixteen-year-old boy who wondered if he would have difficulty getting a driver's license.

In the second study, eighty-seven consecutively discharged women patients were asked four questions designed to reveal feelings of shame and five to discover expectations of discrimination. A combined positive score of 0–3 was deemed a low-stigma score and 4–9 was considered high. Forty women had low scores and forty-seven had high ones. The clustering of single, separated, and divorced respondents in the high group might reflect that group's projection of their relative inability to adjust to the community, as well as the Cummings' theory that resumption of full role participation and integration permits a certain "destigmatization."

In a survey of ninety-one community leaders in the Washington Heights area of New York City, Dohrenwend and his co-workers investigated the leaders' attitudes toward the mentally ill (Dohrenwend, Bernard, and Kolb 1962). Most of the sample came from the four main ethnic groups in the area: Jewish, Negro, Irish, and Puerto Rican. Interviews were obtained with 96 percent of the sample.

The investigators found that the leaders were quite able to identify the six Star vignettes as describing mentally ill people: 100 percent identified the paranoid schizophrenic as mentally ill; 72 percent, the simple schizophrenic; 63 percent, the alcoholic; 51 percent, the juvenile behavior disorder; 49 percent, the anxiety neurotic; and 40 percent, the compulsive phobic.

In their response to social-distance items, 94 percent disagreed with barring a former mental patient from the neighborhood, and 90 percent were willing to accept him as a close friend. Eighty-six percent would sponsor him for membership in their favorite club or rent him a room. Although 55 percent were willing to trust their children with a former mental hospital patient, only 39 percent would not discourage their children from marrying him. Thus, in six of the seven social relationships investigated, a majority of the community leaders refused to put very much social distance between themselves and those who had been mental hospital patients.

Dohrenwend followed up the above-cited study with a survey of the residents of the same area (1966). A subgroup of a population probability sample was selected so that an equal number of household heads were from each of the four main ethnic groups proportionately by educational level. The subsample, including ninety-four married couples and twenty-six single-male household heads, totaled 214 people, of whom 71 percent were actually interviewed. Dohrenwend found that 90 percent of the respondents identified the paranoid schizophrenic as mentally ill; 67 percent, the simple schizophrenic; 41 percent, the alcoholic and the juvenile behavior disorder; 31 percent, the anxiety neurotic; and 24 percent, the compulsive phobic.

Answers to the social-distance questions showed general acceptance of the mentally ill. Of those interviewed, 82 percent disagreed with barring the former mental patient from their neighborhood, while 72 percent were willing to accept him as a close friend. Sixty-seven percent were willing to sponsor him in their favorite club or society; 62 percent, to hire him; and 54 percent, to rent him a room. However, only 27 percent would trust their children to his care, and 37 percent would not discourage their children from marrying him. Thus in the five least-intimate situations, the former mental hospital patient was well accepted, but he was not so welcome as a prospective baby-sitter or son-in-law.

Dohrenwend and Chin-Shong analyzed both of Dohrenwend's studies to test the hypotheses that there had been an increasing acceptance of deviant behavior as mental illness and that there was a greater tolerance of deviance in low-status groups (1967). They concluded that although the public had become better able to identify case descriptions as indicating mental illness, "sharp differences in judgement of the seriousness of the problem remain. While psychiatrists' evaluations center on the amount of the individual's underlying psychopathology, the public tends to judge seriousness in terms of the threat to others" (p. 417).

After examining the recommendations for the treatment of their hypothetical paranoid schizophrenic, Dohrenwend and Chin-Shong reported that the community leaders and those respondents in the general survey with a postgraduate education advised outpatient treatment more often than hospitalization. In contrast, 85 percent of the general-survey respondents with less than a seventh-grade education advocated hospitalization. Thus the recommendations of the less-educated group were closer to the probably expert psychiatric opinion.

Combining this result with the answers to the social-distance questions, the investigators reached their second major conclusion: "The appearance of greater tolerance of deviant behavior in low-status groups is an artifact of viewing their attitudes within a high-status frame of reference. When both lower and upper-status define a pattern of behavior as seriously deviant, lower-status groups are less tolerant. Moreover, the relatively tolerant policy of upper-status groups appears to be the consequence of the generally more liberal orientation rather than of comprehension of the nature of psychopathology in psychiatric terms" (1967, p. 417).

The findings of the two Washington Heights studies also form the substance of a later monograph by Chin-Shong (1968). In it he investigates the similarity "between two phenomena—the way that people respond socially to members of ethnic outgroups and to persons who are or have been mentally ill" (p. 1). From the comparison of reported public attitudes toward ethnic groups with his and Dohrenwend's data, Chin-Shong developed a "theory of threat" as the cause of social rejection.

Assuming public rejection of the mentally ill, Phillips in 1961 explored its dimensions in Branford, Connecticut, a town of 17,000 inhabitants (1964). Taking every fifteenth entry from the address section of the Branford City Directory, he obtained a sample of three hundred married women. Only thirty-seven substitutes were needed to complete three hundred interviews.

Phillips presented his own case description of a normal person and four of Star's vignettes, combined with information about the source of help tnat the described individual was using. These sources included seeking no help, seeing a clergyman, consulting a physician, consulting a psychiatrist, and having been in a mental hospital. The sex of the described person was varied. The respondents were then asked five social-distance questions with the rejection score calculated as the mean number of rejective answers.

In his first paper on this study (1963), Phillips reported that, over the total sample, the rejection score (the mean number of rejections on a five-point social-distance scale) when no help was sought was 1.35; when help was sought from a clergyman, 1.57; from a physician, 1.87; from a psychiatrist, 2.56; and from a mental hospital, 3.04. He noted that the largest difference between adjoining items was from seeing a physician to seeing a psychiatrist. No correlation was apparent between the differential rejection by type of help and age, religion, education, social class, or authoritarian personality of the respondent. However, those respondents who knew a person who had sought help for emotional problems or who disagreed with the norm of self-reliance least rejected people who were seeking help from a physician, followed by those consulting a clergyman, and then by those seeking no help at all. Only 9 percent of those interviewed disagreed with the norm of self-reliance, while 37 percent had either relatives or friends who had sought help for emotional problems.

Phillips concluded that the mentally ill person who seeks help may be rejected by others in the community: "We can easily imagine an individual who, because he fears stigma attached to the help-seeker, does not utilize the professional resource for his problems" (1963, p. 972). Phillips sees the cost of seeking help as rejection by others and a consequently negative self-image. He thus feels that one should balance the gain from psychiatric treatment against the price of seeking help.

In another paper (1964), Phillips analyzed his study's data pertaining to the influence of described deviant behavior on rejection, and the effect of the individual's sex on the rejection suffered. He found that some behavior was more strongly rejected than others, which he correlated with the extent that the behavior was visibly different from role expectations. Also, men were rejected more strongly than women in every category of behavior deviation. Phillips inferred that there is a difference between the public's definition of mental illness and a psychiatrist's definition. He also concluded that the visibility of the destructive behavior of a former mental hospital patient is the major factor in his rejection, rather than the severity of his psychiatric disorder as such. Although his data showed that both sex and the type of help sought were important factors in the rejection of the mentally ill, Phillips found that the differences in described behavior were more important than those of any other of the studied variables, either alone or in combination.

In 1963, the Columbia University School of Public Health and Administrative Medicine and the New York City Community Mental Health Board attempted to assess the feelings of adult New Yorkers about their mental health services (Elinson, Padilla, and Perkins 1967). The survey also explored public conceptions of mental illness and attitudes toward the mentally ill. A systematic selection of 1,500 housing units yielded a random sample of 3,000 people, of whom 87 percent were finally interviewed. The results of this study were similar to those of the Maryland surveys. In the preface to their book, Perkins sees the idea of stigmatization and rejection of the mentally ill as overly simple and outmoded: "The public does not globally reject the mentally ill. On the contrary, the public does have hope for a favorable outcome to treatment of the patient, and accepts the proposition that this should be as near home as possible" (p. x).

The majority of the respondents in this study expressed the belief that mental illness was an illness like other illnesses, that there were many different kinds of mental illness, and that payment for the treatment of mental illness should be included in regular health-insurance coverage. A majority also felt that it was not easy to recognize someone who had once had a serious mental illness, and that little could be done for the mentally ill. Ninety percent wanted the government to raise and spend more money on mental health services.

The researchers found that 80 percent of those interviewed were willing to work with a former mental hospital patient; 64 percent, to hire him; 43 percent, to work under him; and 69 percent, to have him as their neighbor. However, 52 percent would not be willing to agree to his marrying into their family, and 57 percent would not share an apartment with him. It was also reported that "one out of two adults in New York City personally has known someone who has had help for mental or emotional problems. And almost as many New Yorkers admit to having had personal problems themselves for which they could have used help" (p. xiv).

The Kentucky Mental Health Planning Commission studied attitudes toward the mentally ill in preparation for developing statewide community health programs (1964). One thousand people were selected through an area probability sample stratified by urban and rural residences according to the 1960 census. Ninety-seven percent of the sample were interviewed.

Using questions from previous studies such as the one in Baltimore, the authors obtained results similar to those found in Baltimore and New York. An overwhelming majority identified the three Star case descriptions as indicating mental illness, with 94 percent of the respondents advising that the paranoid schizophrenic see a doctor. Ninety-two percent gave the same advice for the simple schizophrenic, and 89 percent similarly agreed for the alcoholic. Ninety-one percent knew that there were many different kinds of mental illness, while 82 percent agreed with seeking psychiatric help when one has strange ideas or behaves oddly. Eighty-nine percent said they would care for a mentally ill member of their family at home if a doctor thought it would not be harmful to the patient.

Social-distance questions elicited that 81 percent of those interviewed were willing to work with a former mental hospital patient; 54 percent, to room with him; and 68 percent, to work in a mental hospital. When asked if they knew anyone who was or had been mentally ill, 67 percent replied affirmatively, with 27 percent referring to relatives and 40 percent to friends or acquaintances.

In 1967, as an adjunct to a five-year development of mental health programs, Edgerton and Bentz, of the Community Psychiatry Section of the Department of Psychiatry at the

University of North Carolina School of Medicine, surveyed a random sample of 960 adults from the two predominantly rural counties which were to be the focus of the programs (1969). A 97 percent response rate was achieved. The sample was primarily rural, poorly educated, and of low socioeconomic status, with a median family income of less than $4,000. Nearly 40 percent of the families had incomes below the $3,000 poverty level. Only 4 percent of the respondents had graduated from college, while 51 percent had not gone beyond the ninth grade. The median age was forty-six years, with 32 percent being urban and 68 percent rural.

The investigators found that their population seemed generally enlightened about mental illness and appeared not to reject the mentally ill out of hand. More than 75 percent of the respondents opposed the idea that little can be done for mental illness or that a mentally ill person can never be normal and healthy again. Seventy-five percent disagreed that few people who enter mental hopitals ever leave, while 65 percent felt that most discharged mental patients would make a good adjustment to the community. Almost everyone interviewed thought that mental illness was an illness like any other, with 87 percent agreeing that a great deal can be done to prevent its occurrence.

Edgerton and Bentz employed social-distance questions similar to those used in the Baltimore study and found that 88 percent of the respondents would be willing to work with someone who had been mentally ill; 67 percent, to rent an apartment to him; 57 percent, to room with him; 44 percent, to conceive of falling in love with him; and 72 percent, to work in a mental hospital. A majority of those interviewed did not perceive mental hospitals as similar to prisons, rejected the proposition that these hospitals were to manage patients rather than to cure patients, and disagreed that little could be done for hospitalized patients except to ensure their personal comfort and regular meals.

Edgerton and Bentz interpreted their findings as further

evidence that public attitudes toward mental illness have been changing favorably. They cited the similarity between their findings and those of Lemkau and Crocetti, while contrasting their results with those of earlier studies, such as the one by the Cummings.

Employer Attitudes Toward the Mentally Ill

In a work-oriented culture, employment plays an important part in the recovery and readjustment of the former mental hospital patient. Therefore, employer attitudes toward the mentally ill can be significant. A number of surveys have attempted to assess employers' knowledge about mental illness and their attitudes about hiring such individuals.

In one of the major studies of this question, Olshansky, Grob, and Malamud investigated a sample of 200 Boston employers, half of whom were manufacturers (1958). Thirteen percent of the sample refused to be interviewed. Of those interviewed, 75 percent stated that they would hire former mental hospital patients as a matter of policy, but most had had limited experience with them and seemed poorly informed about mental illness.

Further interviews with twenty-two industrial physicians and representatives of ten employment agencies and ten unions showed that they too reported little experience with former mental hospital patients and had slight knowledge about mental illness. These data were believed to indicate that discharged mental hospital patients concealed their history from their employers, unions, and employment agencies.

Another somewhat smaller study of Boston-area employers was made by Landy and Griffith of the Massachusetts Mental Health Center (1958). They interviewed fifty-two employers, representing a variety of businesses and professions, and reported that over 77 percent showed "vigorously positive attitudes" toward hiring individuals with a current or past history of mental illness (p. 385). The sincerity of these attitudes was partially tested when thirty-three former mental hospital patients sought employment with twenty-four employers who had stated that they were receptive to the idea and five who had not. Twenty-eight of the thirty-three patients obtained employment: nineteen with the help of vocational counselors and nine through their own efforts. The investigators concluded that "just the fact of emotional illness does not necessarily carry with it an ineradicable stigma insofar as the vocational world is concerned" (p. 390).

Two other studies focused on the former mental hospital patient's on-the-job performance and experience. Margolin surveyed the attitudes of employers who had hired directly from the Veterans Administration hospital in Brockton, Massachusetts (1961). Questionnaires were sent to seventy-three employers, of whom forty-eight or 65 percent, completed the form for seventy-seven employees. The employers were asked to evaluate the former patient's overall performance, to assess his strengths and weaknesses, and to suggest improvements in the work preparation given to patients.

At the time of the study, the length of employment time for the former patients ranged from two weeks to four years, with 35 percent having more than two years' longevity. In general, the former patients were found to be as skillful as other employees with similar jobs. The unskilled workers had the greatest employment instability. Margolin concluded that a discharged mental hospital patient's preparedness and competence seemed more important in obtaining and holding a job than employer attitudes.

Whatley's Columbia, South Carolina, survey was designed to test the hypothesis that "intolerant, unfavorable attitudes toward mental illness and its associated residual manifestations among ex-patients would tend toward early dismissal or resignation" (1964, p. 121). The aim of the questionnaire was to discover the importance to the employer of an employee's history of mental hospitalization and the range of employer tolerance of inappropriate, unwarranted, or undesirable on-the-job behavior.

The sample population consisted of one hundred employers who had hired discharged patients. Of these, fifty-four knew of their employees' hospitalization, while the other forty-six either were unaware of the hospitalization or were unwilling to admit such knowledge. Job longevity was the principal criterion used in assessing the impact of employer beliefs and attitudes on the discharged patients' vocational adjustment. Half of the respondents had employed the former patients for nine months or longer and half for less than nine months. Despite the thorny technical and statistical problems of analysis, it appeared that the long-term employers were, as a group, better educated, more amenable to hiring former mental hospital patients, and more tolerant of annoying or irregular behavior on the job. Whatley concluded that "ex-patients who succeed in concealing their illness are unlikely to avert unwanted consequences of maladaptive symptoms carried over to the job. These residues often invite unwelcome disfavor with the employer, whether or not he is aware of their clinical origin. This conclusion obviously reaffirms the value of interpreting symptomatic deviations to employers in educational and placement procedures aimed at cultivating greater receptivity towards prospective ex-patient employees" (p. 130).

Factors Affecting Attitudes Toward the Mentally Ill

Many factors have been examined for correlation with attitudes toward the mentally ill. This section reviews the reported attitudinal effects of the respondent's age, sex, marital status, ethnicity, education, prior social or familial ties to the mentally ill, and personality.

The consensus is that young people are least likely to reject the mentally ill, with Woodward (1951), the Cummings (1957), Freeman (1961), Whatley (1959), Phillips (1964), and Crocetti and Lemkau (1963) among those who support this finding. Chin-Shong stated that age was "the strongest single predictor of rejection" (1968, p. 89). He also noted that this effect decreased with education and leadership status (pp. 84-90).

Sex has not generally been correlated with attitudes toward the mentally ill. However, when Chin-Shong reported some interaction effect with ethnicity and age on social-distance questions, he found older women more rejective than older men and black women more rejective than black men (1968, p. 95).

Married persons are often considered more conservative than single, and Whatley found a slightly greater acceptance of the mentally ill among his single respondents than the married ones. But his results also indicated that the divorced and separated were more rejective than either married or single individuals. He suggested that the personalities most susceptible to divorce might also be those most likely to reject the mentally ill (1959).

Blacks have been found to have a more negative response to the mentally ill than whites in the researches of Ramsey and Siepp (1948), Crawford, Rollins, and Sutherland (1960), and Whatley (1959). Although these studies did not intercorrelate ethnicity with age or sex, black women were noted above as particularly rejective of the mentally ill.

As early as 1938, Davis pointed out that the better educated are more accepting of the mentally ill on humanistic and liberal grounds rather than because of any enlightened or scientific understanding of psychopathology. The literature shows strong agreement that better-educated people tend to be more enlightened and more scientific about mental illness. These attributes are often considered to lead to a greater acceptance of the mentally ill. Positive correlations between education and acceptance of former mental hospital patients or those who have been mentally ill are reported by Ramsey and Siepp (1948), Woodward (1951), the Cummings (1957), Whatley (1959), Lemkau and Crocetti (1962), and Phillips (1964). However, Dohrenwend and Chin-Shong found that education has only a small negative correlation with rejection (1967), while Freeman and Kassebaum found little relation (1960), and Nunnally none (1961).

There is evidence that social interaction can reduce social

distance in some situations (Knight 1968). Altrocchi and Eisdorfer found that although college and nursing-school upperclassmen acquired more positive attitudes toward the mentally ill after training that included contact with psychiatric patients, education that merely increased the students' information about mental illness did not change their attitudes (1961). Chin-Shong reported that acquaintance with a psychiatric outpatient did not lead to greater acceptance of the mentally ill, but that a close tie with an inpatient did (1968). Phillips also noted that attitudinal distance was reduced if a friend had been mentally ill, and was further lessened in the case of an ill relative (1964). Whatley, however, found no relation between social distance and acquaintance with the mental patient (1959).

The dynamic interpretation of prejucice, best exemplified in Bettelheim and Janowitz (1950), finds the prejudiced person using prejudice to satisfy his own psychological needs. Certain personalities, such as the "authoritarian personality" described by Adorno et al. (1950), are more likely to use prejudice than others. Nudelman (1965) and Mulfad (1968) are among those who have pointed out the likelihood of such personalities rejecting the mentally ill, and Ackerman has stated that being prejudiced is itself a sign of mental illness (1965). Whatley's findings that individuals with broken marriages are more rejective of the mentally ill than either married or single people could support these ideas.

On the other hand, Goffman has argued that a known former patient should be more accepting of other former mental patients because they all share the same stigma and are therefore part of the same group (1963). However, Chin-Shong's "theory of threat" indicated that a former mental hospital patient would be the most threatening to a person with the severest psychopathology, who would have the greatest fear of being overwhelmed by it. Since none of the studies reviewed include a follow-up psychiatric evaluation of those respondents most rejective of the mentally ill, no direct evidence is available on the correlation between such rejection and personality factors.

Summary and Conclusions

Some two dozen studies have been reviewed here. The findings are quite disparate. Many of the studies report that the public or employers are poorly informed about mental illness, but many others report them well informed. Several writers find a great deal of social distance between the public and the mentally ill, but others find much less. Some researchers conclude that the public is unable to identify mental illness, but others conclude it is quite able to do so. Some investigators see the public's attitudes as hard to change or even necessarily rejective, but others claim that these attitudes have already changed. The list could be much longer.

Although public attitudes toward the mentally ill have generally been reported as more positive since 1960, the chronology itself is not the underlying issue. Several earlier researchers, such as Star and the Cummings, concluded from their findings that the public's attitude toward the mentally ill was one of stigmatization, rejection, and, in essence, prejudice. The Cummings, as noted previously, saw the rejection of the mentally ill as necessary for "the reaffirmation of the solidarity of the social system" (1957, p. 127). If stigmatization and rejection are necessary concomitants to mental illness, such attitudes should be very strong and pervasive. Accordingly, the rather positive findings of Freeman and Simmons; Lemkau and Crocetti; M. Lemkau; Meyer; Elinson, Padilla, and Perkins; Edgerton and Bentz; and the Kentucky Mental Health Planning Commission bring the idea of "necessary" or "strong" rejection and stigmatization into question.

The next chapter attempts to outline the theoretical explanations and interpretations that have been advanced to support the ideas that public attitudes toward the mentally ill are, necessarily, characterized by stigmatization, rejection, or prejudice. Such a sharpening of the issues should allow the formulation of specific testable hypotheses.

CHAPTER 2

Theoretical Background

Before reviewing the various theoretical issues raised by different researchers about the nature of public attitudes toward the mentally ill, it may be helpful to examine and more fully define several of the concepts referred to in these studies. The terms *attitude, stigma,* and *prejudice* were used in the previous chapter without any explicit definitions. Such definitions will now be presented with an outline of the concept of stereotypy. A discussion of some of the theories mentioned above will follow.

Conceptualizing Negative Attitudes

Prejudice and *negative stereotypy* are terms used to describe persistent clusters of negative attitudes usually associated with behavior such as rejection and stigmatization. An *attitude* itself may be seen as "the individual's organization of psychological processes, as inferred from his behavior" (Newcomb in Gould and Kolb 1964, pp. 40–41). Taking a psychological position, Krech and Crutchfield suggest that "an attitude can be defined as an enduring organization of motivational, emotional, perceptual, and cognitive processes with respect to some aspect of the individual's world" (1948, p. 152). From a sociological vantage, attitudes may be regarded as the individual's counterpart of social values. Thus, although they may be measured by such cognitive exchanges as interviews, attitudes ultimately refer to behavior.

Writing in the *Dictionary of the Social Sciences,* Jahoda defines prejudice as "a negative, unfavourable attitude toward a group or its individual members; it is characterized by stereotyped beliefs; the attitude results from processes within the bearer of the attitude rather than from reality testing of the attributes of the group in question" (Gould and Kolb 1964, pp. 527-28). She states that in the social sciences the term prejudice is used almost exclusively in relation to ethnic groups and refers to Harding and others who define prejudice as simply "an unfavorable ethnic attitude" (Harding et al. 1964, p. 1022). Jahoda notes the criticism by Cattell (1948, p. 195) and others of the introduction of the term prejudice into systematic social science and warns of the "importance of clear definitions in this area to which implicit value judgements could indeed be easily introduced" (p. 528).

The term *stereotype,* when used in medicine, connotes persistent repetition of senseless words, acts, or movements. Over fifty years ago, Lippman (1922) introduced the sociological concept of *stereotypy* as preconceived ideas and beliefs about the external world which serve to increase economy of thought. Usage was then gradually narrowed until stereotypy became "an exaggerated belief associated with a category. Its function is to justify (rationalize) our conduct with respect to that category" (Allport 1954, p. 187). Jahoda gives a somewhat fuller definition of stereotype as "beliefs about classes of individuals, groups, or objects, which are 'preconceived', i.e. resulting not from fresh appraisals of each phenomenon but from routinized habits of judgement and expectation" (in Gould and Kolb 1964, p. 694). After distinguishing stereotype, through its neutrality, from prejudice, she adds that "the stereotype is a belief which is not held as an hypothesis buttressed by evidence but rather is mistaken whole or in part for established fact" (p. 694). Merton notes that social scientists see stereotypes as beliefs which are free from affect or evaluation (1957, pp. 426-27).

Ackerman speaks of prejudice as the fear of the unknown

and contends that "it is the tenacious refusal to know and to trust the other that breeds prejudice" (1965, p. 27). He argues that any definition of prejudice must consider both intrapsychic and interpersonal forces since "the root of the prejudicial attitude is its antihuman quality. It is the urge to destroy the humanness of the other person" (p. 31). Thus, "people tending toward mental illness are prone to lean on prejudice" (p. 33).

The origins of such strong negative feelings toward the prejudicial object have been explored by Adorno et al. (1950) and by Bettelheim and Janowitz (1950). To very briefly summarize their findings on this point, prejudice is a hostile and deprecatory attitude toward a group or toward an individual because he is a member of that group. It may or may not conform to prevailing social attitudes. Education and experience, which demonstrate the irrationality of these attitudes, may modify or eradicate this type of prejudice. However, once prejudice serves a psychological function for a person, he clings tenaciously to it and to its basic tenets unquestioningly. It becomes a dogmatic conceptual framework which he rigidly adheres to and which he applies to his daily existence. Since this type of prejudice makes him psychologically secure, he maintains it even at the expense of his habits of rational criticism. The prejudiced person does not question the rationale for his prejudice and does not see the need either for its justification or for its modification. Thus, prejudice consists of basic tenets which cannot be proved or refuted because of their emotional value to the bearer.

A variety of true and false qualities are attributed to the object of the prejudice. He is seen as possessing in particular those universal instincts most subject to social controls, particularly excessive sexual and aggressive drives. He becomes a storehouse of these and other repressed drives of the prejudiced person. Therefore, the more morally rigid and less psychologically aware a person is, the more likely he is to project his own "darker side" onto others as prejudice in an effort to control it. The unacceptable component of the self must be projected onto a person who has distinctive qualities which identify him as separate. The logic of this explanation and of the development of prejudice is the same, whether psychological need is a unique clinical one or simply an individual instance of a global need, such as the need for predictable social intercourse.

The prejudiced person's need to think in stereotyped terms about a group may be conceptualized with Sullivan's formulation of selective attention and selective inattention to all information about the group (1956). The concept of focal awareness was explored and expanded by Meldman (1970). In relation to social roles, prejudice may be supported and enhanced by the selection of peers and authority figures who share the same particular prejudice.

A person with a psychologically rewarding, and therefore stereotyping, prejudice will clearly want to put as much social distance as possible between himself and the objects of his prejudice. Not only do they represent all that he fears and represses, but true, equal personal contact with them would make it more difficult to maintain the prejudice. Thus, those identifiable as members of the group against which there is prejudice will be stigmatized, rejected, and avoided.

In medicine, the term *stigma* applies to any mark or peculiarity which aids in identification or diagnosis, but in the social sciences it always has a negative connotation. Goffman defines stigma as an attribute that is deeply discrediting (1963). The bearer of the stigma is seen as a person who is victimized, rejected, or discriminated against solely because he possesses a particular trait (that trait being the stigma).

In the broadest possible sense, anyone is "stigmatized" whenever he attempts any form of social intercourse and is rebuffed because of some attributed group characteristic. For example, a person is stigmatized if his prospective in-laws withdraw their approval upon learning his religion, or if his hotel reservation is not honored when his race is discovered, or if excellent secretarial training cannot overcome the effects of obesity in obtaining employment. In a socially stratified society with as great a variety of religions and races as the United States, the possibilities for stigmatization are almost limitless.

It is therefore important to consider the degree of stigmatization. This can be done in terms of the frequency with which rejection is encountered at different levels of social intimacy. A Jewish Negro may not be welcome in a white Protestant home. He might, however, be invited if he were only Jewish, but even then he might not be accepted as a son-in-law. The Negro might thus be considered more stigmatized than the Jew, although both have suffered rejection.

Social scientists tend to use the term stigma when the social rejection is rather frequent and rather severe. This is especially the case when it is applied to members of weaker or minority groups where the dominant group utilizes claims of moral, intellectual, or other superiority in exploiting or oppressing the weaker group.

In sum, a negative attitude toward an identifiable group and its members may harden into an unquestionable, uncriticizable set of preconceived or stereotyped opinions when prejudice can fulfill a psychological need in a person. Possession of such a stereotyping prejudice will lead an individual to stigmatize the group he is prejudiced against and to keep its members at the maximum possible social distance.

The Theory of Rejection

The preceding discussion makes it clear that the issue of the stigmatization of the mentally ill can be seen as two related questions. First, is there a generally negative attitude or simple prejudice against the mentally ill? Secondly, if so, is the nature of mental illness in society such that a negative attitude toward the mentally ill will serve for certain individuals an important psychological need which would change the simple prejudice into a stereotyping prejudice and lead to the stigmatization and severe rejection of the mentally ill?

Two concepts that have often been important in theories about the rejection or acceptance of the mentally ill are social deviance and the social role prescribed for those who are ill. The latter is usually referred to as the *sick role.*

The *Dictionary of the Social Sciences* (pp. 196-97) offers two definitions of *deviant behavior.* The first is essentially the statistical one of behavior which varies widely from the norm. Many types of mental illness could produce such behavior. The second definition, taken from Cohen in *Sociology Today,* describes deviant behavior as "behavior which violates institutionalized expectations—that is, expectations which are shared and recognized as legitimate within a social system" (in Merton, Broom, and Cottrell 1959, p. 462). Thus, "we here define deviant behavior in terms of the relationship of action to institutionalized expectations, not in terms of its relationship to personality structure. Behavior which is psychotic, neurotic, maladjusted or otherwise pathological from a psychiatric or mental hygiene point of view . . . is not, as such, subject matter for the sociology of deviant behavior" (pp. 463-64).

However, it is possible to argue that the exclusion of psychopathological behavior applies to sociological theories rather than to understanding public attitudes toward the mentally ill; that is, at least some of the pathological behavior of the mentally ill might be seen by society as deviant even though its causation may be personal and psychological rather than sociological. This view makes any equivalence between social deviance and psychopathological behavior much more complicated. It is the social expectations that are the standard, not a simple average behavior pattern. Even if only common social roles are considered, the range of expected behavior is enormous and its acceptability can turn on a rather small factor.

For example, if a man arrives at a party, hangs up his coat, greets his hostess, and pinches her, she will probably be offended. If, however, he arrives, hangs up his coat, has several drinks, and then greets and pinches his hostess, she is much less likely to be offended. This difference stems from the difference between the social expectations about a man not completely in control of his actions and those about the same man under "normal" circumstances.

Where deviancy is related to social expectations, the sick role becomes the potentially most important means for the mentally ill to have their behavior tolerated. The sick role thus may be seen as an "excuse" for deviant behavior under certain circumstances.

Merton and others have developed a systematic typology of social actions in which deviant behavior originates from institutionalized strain and inconsistent social structure (1957). Deviancy is seen as logically subject to the same mechanisms of social control as nondeviant behavior. When deviant behavior is viewed as the violation of institutionalized expectations, the two extremes of deviancy are the rebel, who actively violates expectations, and the totally withdrawn individual, who violates these by nonparticipation.

Parsons conceives the sick role as closely resembling the withdrawn deviant (1958). He finds five criteria for invoking the sick role:

1. There is a disturbance of capacity with reference to social-role performance in the case of mental illness and task performance in the case of physical illness.
2. There is an exemption from the usual social-role obligations.
3. The patient is not held personally responsible for his state.
4. The illness state with its attendant incapacity is legitimized so long as it is clearly recognized that it is intrinsically an undesirable state and is to be recovered from as expeditiously

as possible (conditional legitimation).

5. There must be acceptance of the need for help and of the obligation to cooperate with the source of the help (pp. 182–83).

The last two criteria make the patient's will to get better an important factor. In the mentally ill the sick role's excusal from social-role performance would depend on the acceptance of the obligations of the sick role. It is, therefore, conceivable that the sick role may be denied when the patient's attitude or history is seen as inappropriate. This is illustrated by the hostile reception accorded those who consciously produce factitious signs of illness as part of the disorder called Munchausen's syndrome (Spiro 1968).

Parsons relates this question to the mentally ill by noting that "a larger component of the phenomena of mental illness presumably operates through motivation and is hence related to the problems and mechanisms of social control." Therefore, "the fact of this orientation of the society militates against any orientation which would be inclined to let individuals 'rest on their oars', but puts very much of a premium on the protection and development of capacity" (1958, p. 181).

Another related difficulty in applying the sick role to the mentally ill is the issue of chronicity. Since the legitimation of the deviancy is conditional on the patient's getting well as fast as he can, a chronic condition with a poor prognosis for significant recovery could change the role given the patient from a sick role to that of a cripple or invalid. Such a role carries with it at least some circumscription of social acceptance and respectability.

A restaurant owner highly conscious of "Typhoid Mary" might well, if wrongly, refuse to hire a former typhoid fever patient if he saw the disease as incurable. The same person might have few qualms about employing a former bank robber despite the obvious stigma if he believed the ex-thief to be rehabilitated. Thus the historical professional assertions of some mental illnesses' incurability, such as Kraepelin's concept of *dementia praecox* (1919), could affect the application of the sick role to the mentally ill.

Accordingly, at least some mental illnesses might be equated with social deviance either directly or as behavior violating institutionalized expectations where such exculpatory privileges as the sick role are denied. Whenever psychopathological behavior is, in fact, seen as equivalent to deviant behavior, it would naturally be subjected to the normal social controls appropriate to the deviant behavior it most resembles. This is essentially what the Cummings, Star, and Clausen have argued. Thus, for example, the Cummings write:

> Society must at all times remain in some kind of equilibrium or it loses its integrity and ceases to be a system. As we have said earlier, the fundamental basis of this equilibrium in a stable society, is the members' desire to act most of the time in the way that is expected of them. This complimentarity of expectations is disrupted in mental illness; the effective person appears no longer to be governed by the norms which apply to his fellows. He seems insensitive to the expectations of those around him. He has, therefore, in a very real and crucial way, broken his ties with society. He appears no longer to be bound by the expectations which govern the rest of us; he has slipped out of the web of obligations, and therefore he poses a problem of control. The need for control raises the question, can a member of society break the rules and not be punished? All societies punish deviants in one way or another, because the implications of not punishing them threaten the stability of society. As the great sociologist, Emile Durkheim, perceived, it is not entirely to punish the criminal that punitive action is taken, but rather to allow the remaining members to reassure one another that they are members of a society, which is safe from deviant tendencies. (Cumming and Cumming 1957, p. 99)

The Cummings' last point recalls the definition of an attitude as an individual counterpart of social values. Here, the social value of having a predictable, reliable society becomes an individual negative attitude toward the mentally ill—an attitude which necessarily serves important individual psychological needs.

Star outlines her concept of the popular view of mental illness:

> According to this view of man, rationality and the ability to exercise self-control are essential, basic human qualities. From this it follows that he acts and his acts are reasonable—appropriate to the circumstances in which he finds himself and are intelligible to others, in light of the circumstances. Given this view of normalcy it follows quite consistently that if mental illness represents the loss of normalcy or its opposite, it must necessarily turn out to be a rather extreme form of psychosis. Given this orientation, it also follows that mental illness is a very threatening, fearful thing, and not an idea to be entertained lightly about anyone. Emotionally, it represents to people the loss of what they consider to be the distinctively human qualities of rationality and free will, and there is a kind of horror in dehumanization. As both our data and other studies make clear, mental illness is something that people want to keep as far from themselves as possible. (Star 1957, p. 5)

Clausen feels that the behavioral manifestations and interpersonal consequences of severe mental disorder seem sufficiently different from those of physical illness to insure that the mentally ill will not easily be accorded the sick role. He notes that even psychiatrists and nurses, who do subscribe to the view that mental disorder is to be treated as illness, tend in their casual remarks to use "mental illness" as a devaluing term (1959).

The use of "dehumanization" and the argument that the public seeks maximum possible social distance from the mentally ill parallel the earlier discussion of a stereotyping prejudice. This stereotyping prejudice against the mentally ill is triggered by a basic social value and an individual psychological need. Therefore, this approach leaves no doubt that the mentally ill will be rejected. Indeed, it is the lack of even more severe reaction that the Cummings (1957) find in need of explanation:

However, it has become untenable to punish the mentally ill, the modern rational, scientific approach has led us to define the mentally ill person as a sick person, and the question then becomes: Is it right to punish the sick? This is the dilemma which people face when they attempt to make up their minds about mental illness, this is one dilemma that the pattern of denial, isolation and insulation helps to resolve. (p. 124)

First, denial of mental illness; second, isolation of the affected person in a hospital, when mental illness can no longer be denied; and finally, insulation of the whole vexing problem by secondary denial that the problem exists insofar as it needs solving by ordinary citizens. (pp. 122–23)

The final report of the Joint Commission on Mental Illness and Health (1961) also argues this "theory of rejection," as it will be referred to in this book:

As a reaction to deviant behavior, rejection is, of course, a well established characteristic of any social group. Society depends on a system of order, conformity, solidarity; it uses rejection as a threat to exact thorough individual compliance with the expectations of the group. We believe that peculiar significance of the typical person's feelings towards a madman has been widely overlooked, even by social scientists, as a key reason for the lag in hardhitting efforts to provide decent care for the mentally ill. (p. 58)

The nonconformist—whether he be a foreigner or an "oddball," intellectual or idiot, genius or jester, individualist or hobo, physically or mentally abnormal—pays a penalty for "being different," unless his peculiarity is considered acceptable for his particular group, or unless he lives in a place or period of particularly high tolerance and enlightenment. A socially visible characteristic of the psychotic person is that he becomes a stranger among his own people. (p. 59)

Mental illness is different from physical in the one fundamental aspect that it tends to disturb and repel others rather than evoke their sympathy and desire to help. (p. 84)

Conclusions

This chapter has explored the development of negative attitudes toward a group and its members into strong prejudices. When the negative attitudes fill a psychological need for their holder, they become stereotyped and unquestionable—in short, a hardened prejudice. A person bearing such a prejudice will stigmatize and strongly reject any representative of that prejudice and seek to maintain maximum possible social distance from him.

The relationship between psychopathological behavior and the concepts of social deviance and the sick role has been examined as a preliminary to presenting the theory advanced by the Cummings, Star, and Clausen about public attitudes toward the mentally ill, or the "theory of rejection' as it is called in this book.

In outline, the "theory of rejection" is as follows: Society needs stability. Therefore, deviance from its social norms, institutionalized or *de facto,* is threatening to both the society and the individual. Psychopathological behavior is a form of social deviance which is not entitled to the sick role and thus is subject to social controls appropriate to exhibited behavior. As social deviance, it is viewed negatively. This leads to negative attitudes toward the mentally ill which are reinforced both by strong individual psychological needs and by the necessity for promoting social predictability. Therefore, the negative attitudes will become stereotyped and a hardened prejudice will develop. The object of the prejudice, the mentally ill person, will be stigmatized and strongly rejected through denial, insulation, and the maintenance of extreme social distance. Furthermore, the universality of the triggering individual psychological need for social reliability insures that the stigmatization and rejection of the mentally ill must be both severe and widespread.

If the "theory of rejection" is correct, there must be a strong and pervasive stigmatization and rejection of mental illness and the mentally ill. It would be reasonable to expect that systematic investigation of the public's attitudes and feelings should therefore show that the public will:

1. Avoid seeing descriptions of emotional disturbance as evidence of mental illness
2. Deny personal experience and contact with mental illness among family and friends
3. Have a stereotyped view of the mentally ill as "dangerous" and fear-provoking
4. Deny that the mentally ill are "sick" or require a physician's care
5. Reject social intimacy with the mentally ill

These propositions are necessary corollaries of the "theory of rejection." Hypotheses 1 will be tested in chapter 3; hypothesis 2, in chapter 4; hypotheses 3 and 4, in chapter 5; and hypothesis 5 in chapters 6–8.

PART II

The Data

CHAPTER 3

Public Identification of the Mentally Ill

In the previous section the literature on the public's attitudes toward the mentally ill has been surveyed, and a "theory of rejection" of the mentally ill has been outlined. Five corollaries of this theory were brought out as hypotheses. This section will present data relating to these hypotheses from our 1960 general survey of a portion of the population in Baltimore, Maryland (hereafter referred to as the Baltimore study) and our 1968 and 1970 studies of members of the United Automobile Workers of America in the Baltimore area (hereafter jointly referred to as the UAW study or individually as Wave I or Wave II of same). The data relevant to each hypothesis will be presented chapter by chapter and then discussed along with data from other researchers. (The basic methodological and theoretical relationship between the data and the hypothesis under consideration is given in each chapter. Further methodological information, such as population characteristics and questionnaire design, and other aspects of the design and execution of the surveys and the processing of the data are discussed in detail in Appendix D.)

There is a prevalent belief that the public cannot or will not acknowledge that a man is mentally ill unless he is a raving lunatic. The corollary is that mental illness infers highly disruptive and distasteful behavior. In this context the phrase *mental illness* becomes an epithet.

Does the public avoid identifying evidence of psychological disturbance as mental illness? Star indicates that the public recognizes little mental illness:

The typical reaction to psychiatry is that anybody who needs psychiatric treatment should see psychiatrists, but that practically no one ever needs psychiatric treatment. If you focus only on the first statement there is public acceptance of psychiatry, but the sphere in which psychiatry was thought relevant . . . was so constricted that we might as well call it public rejection of psychiatry. (Star 1957, p. 3)

Thus knowledge of the public capacity to identify mental illness is important in understanding public attitudes toward mental illness and toward psychiatry.

Methodology

Surveys by Star and by the Cummings in the early 1950s, using the six, now classic, case descriptions developed by Star, showed that only the paranoid schizophrenic was identified as mentally ill by a majority of the respondents. Each vignette described an individual with a different mental illness and was followed by a series of questions to determine whether the respondent thought the person was mentally ill. These case descriptions have become virtually standard devices for measuring public information about, and attitudes toward, the mentally ill. The complete, original texts are presented below:

1. *Paranoid schizophrenic:* I'm thinking of a man—let's call him Frank Jones—who is very suspicious; he doesn't trust anybody, and he's sure that everybody is against him. Sometimes he thinks that people he sees on the street are talking about him or following him around. A couple of times, now, he has beaten up men who didn't even know him. The other night, he began to curse his wife terribly; then he hit her and threatened to kill her because, he said, she was working against him, too, just like everyone else.
2. *Simple schizophrenic:* Now here's a young woman in her twenties, let's call her Betty Smith . . . she has never

had a job, and she doesn't want to go out and look for one. She is a very quiet girl; she doesn't talk much to anyone—even her own family—and she acts like she is afraid of people, especially young men her own age. She won't go out with anyone, and whenever someone comes to visit her family, she stays by herself and daydreams all the time, and shows no interest in anything or anybody.

3. *Anxiety neurotic:* Here's another kind of man; we can call him George Brown. He has a good job and is doing pretty well at it. Most of the time he gets along all right with people, but he is always very touchy and he always loses his temper quickly, if things aren't going his way, or if people find fault with him. He worries a lot about little things, and he seems to be moody and unhappy all the time. Everything is going along all right for him, but he can't sleep nights, brooding about the past, and worrying about things that might go wrong.

4. *Alcoholic:* How about Bill Williams? He never seems to be able to hold a job very long, because he drinks so much. Whenever he has money in his pocket, he goes on a spree; he stays out till all hours drinking, and never seems to care what happens to his wife and children. Sometimes he feels very bad about the way he treats his family; he begs his wife to forgive him and promises to stop drinking, but he always goes off again.

5. *Compulsive phobic:* Here's a different sort of girl—let's call her Mary White. She seems happy and cheerful; she's pretty, has a good job, and is engaged to marry a nice young man. She has loads of friends; everybody likes her, and she's always busy and active. However, she just can't leave the house without going back to see whether she left the gas stove lit or not. And she always goes back again just to make sure she locked the door. And one other thing about her; she's afraid to ride up and down in elevators; she just won't go any place where she'd have to ride in an elevator to get there.

6. *Juvenile character disorder:* Now, I'd like to describe a twelve-year-old boy—Bobby Grey. He's bright enough and in good health, and he comes from a comfortable home. But his father and mother have found out that he's been telling lies for a long time now. He's been stealing things from stores, and taking money from his mother's purse, and he has been playing truant, staying away from school whenever he can. His parents are very upset about the way he acts, but he pays no attention to them. (From original Star questionnaire, also cited in Dohrenwend and Chin-Shong 1967, pp. 418–19)

Findings

In our Baltimore study three of these case descriptions were used (tables 1, 2, and 3). All three were identified as indicative of mental illness by a substantial majority of the respondents, and half of those interviewed were able to identify all three cases as mentally ill. An additional 34 percent identified two cases, while 12 percent could identify only one case and 4 percent could not identify any of the cases as mentally ill.

We found a significant positive correlation between educational attainment and correct identification of the case descriptions as indicative of mental illness (the tables for these and other data cited in the text are in Appendix B). Age also influences the ability to recognize mental illness. Both the under-twenty and over-seventy age groups identify fewer cases

TABLE 1. Identification of Three Examples of Mental Illness (Baltimore, 1960)

	Identified as Mentally Ill	Not Identified as Mentally Ill
Paranoid schizophrenic	91%	9%
Simple schizophrenic	78	22
Alcoholic	62	38

NOTE: N = 1,738.

as mentally ill than the others. However, in all groups at least 75 percent of the respondents identified two or more of the cases.

The ability to identify mental illness seems related to sex, with women doing significantly better than men. Family income is also positively correlated with the ability to identify vignettes of the mentally ill.

Type of birthplace is positively correlated with this ability. Respondents born in a city or town identify significantly more mental illness than those born on a farm. Nevertheless, 81 percent of those born on a farm identified two or more of the case descriptions as mental illness. Marital status and length of residence in Baltimore were also analyzed but were not found to be significantly related to the ability to identify mental illness.

Race alone is not correlated with the identification of mental illness, as both of the races surveyed, white and black, show virtually identical patterns of identification. We analyzed both by race and by social position the number of vignettes identified as indicative of mental illness. Social position was determined by the Hollingshead classification outlined in the "Two-Factor Index of Social Position" (1957) (see appendix table 20 for a description of the classes). Overall class III was the most able to identify mental illness. The somewhat different re-

TABLE 2. Number of Examples of Mental Illness Correctly Identified (Baltimore, 1960)

Number of Cases Identified		Percentage of Respondents
3		50.0%
2		34.0
1		12.0
0		4.0
	Total	100.0%

NOTE: Mean number of cases identified: 2.30; N = 1,738.

TABLE 3. Number of Examples of Mental Illness Correctly Identified, by Contact with Mentally Ill (Baltimore, 1960)

Contact[a]	Number in Sample	Total Percentage	Number of Examples Identified				Mean Number of Examples Identified	Standard Deviation
			Three	Two	One	None		
Have known	1,099	100.0%	53.0%	35.0%	10.0	2.0%	2.39	0.76
Never known	621	100.0	46.1	34.3	15.3	4.3	2.22	0.85
Don't know	18	100.0	22.0	22.0	—	56.0	1.11	1.29
Total	1,738							

NOTE: $p < .01$.

a. Question asked: "Have you ever known anyone who was in a hospital because of mental illness?"

sponses of the races within each social position are discussed below.

When the respondents were asked if they had "ever known anyone who was in a hospital because of mental illness," 63 percent said they had, 36 percent had not, and 1 percent were not sure. Prior contact with mental illness did significantly correlate with the ability to identify mental illness (table 3), yet more than 80 percent of those disclaiming any previous contact with mental hospital patients were able to identify two or more of the case descriptions as indicative of mental illness. The question of contact with the mentally ill is treated more fully in chapter 4.

All three of the Star case descriptions presented were identified as indicative of mental illness by a substantial majority of the respondents, with 84 percent identifying two or more. The demographic variables of age, sex, education, social class, family income, and type of birthplace were found to be significantly related to the ability to identify mental illness, as was previous contact with current or former mental hospital patients. Race, marital status, and mobility were not related to identification ability.

Couch and Kenniston (1960) have raised the general issue of possible "yea-saying" by poorly educated black respondents. We found a significant difference between poorly educated blacks and the rest of the sample. The difference is in the opposite direction from what would be expected if "yea-saying" was playing an important role in the results. These poorly educated respondents identify significantly fewer examples as mentally ill than does the rest of the population. It is of extreme interest to note, however, that even among this group 77 percent are able to identify more than just the paranoid schizophrenic as mentally ill. Thus this study, like Dohrenwend's 1967 study, finds that "yea-saying" is minimal on this topic.

Star and the Cummings found a majority of their study populations unable to identify more than the paranoid schizophrenic vignette as indicative of mental illness. Such data seem to indicate that the public avoids seeing evidence of mental illness. Our Baltimore study finds a majority of the public able to identify as mentally ill all three of the case descriptions used. This conflicts with the findings of Star and the Cummings.

The conflict in the data can be put in some perspective by considering the results of all nine of the studies that have used various of the Star case descriptions (table 4). The work of Star and the Cummings was done in the early 1950s while the other studies are from the period 1960 to 1965. (Elinson, Padilla, and Perkins are not included because they used abbreviated versions of the vignettes [1967]. However, their results are quite similar to the later studies as far as the identification of psychoses is concerned.)

This table clearly shows that the findings reported by Star were replicated by the Cummings but have not been replicated in any study since the early fifties. The percentage identifying the paranoid schizophrenic as mentally ill was increased a minimum of 14 percent over Star's data and 20 percent over the Cummings'. Where Star and the Cummings found only 34 percent and 36 percent of their respective respondents able to identify the simple schizophrenic as mentally ill, succeeding studies did not find less than 67 percent able to do so. The only later survey which had less than a majority identifying the alcoholic as mentally ill was Dohrenwend's 1966 study. Even so, his 41 percent identification is 12 percent higher than Star and 16 percent higher than the Cummings, while the Baltimore survey, the next lowest, had 62 percent.

Dohrenwend (1966) was the only later researcher to use the vignettes about the anxiety neurotic, the juvenile character disorder, and the compulsive phobic. He found increased identification for all of them, ranging from a 50 percent increase for the anxiety neurotic to almost triple the percentage for the juvenile character disorder. His lowest percentage of identification of a vignette as indicative of mental illness was

TABLE 4. Identification of Examples of Mental Illness in Various Populations, by Type of Illness

			Type of Case Identified					
Place	Date	N	Paranoid Schizo-phrenic	Simple Schizo-phrenic	Alcoholic	Anxiety Neurotic	Juvenile Character Disorder	Compulsive Phobic
National[a]	1950	3,500	75%	34%	29%	18%	14%	7%
Blackfoot, Canada[b]	1951	540	69	36	25	20	4	4
Baltimore[c]	1960	1,738	91	78	62	—	—	—
Washington Heights, Manhattan[d]	1960	87	100	72	63	50	50	40
Carroll County[e]	1962	139	95	—	—	—	—	—
Easton[f]	1962	100	89	77	63	—	—	—
Kentucky[g]	1964	970	92	75	75	—	—	—
Washington Heights, Manhattan[h]	1966	151	90	67	41	31	41	24
Saskatchewan, Canada[i]	1965	130	95	67	71	—	—	—

NOTE: All cases were hypothetical.

a. Star 1955a, 1955b, 1957.

b. Cumming and Cumming 1957.

c. Crocetti and Lemkau 1963.

d. Dohrenwend, Bernard, and Kolb 1962. Sample of community leaders only.

e. M. Lemkau 1962.

f. Meyer 1964.

g. Kentucky Mental Health Planning Commission 1964.

h. Dohrenwend and Chin-Shong 1967; Dohrenwend 1966.

i. Rootman and Lafare 1965.

the 24 percent for the compulsive phobic, which is higher than that reported by either Star or the Cummings for half of their case descriptions. It is also only slightly less than what the Cummings and Star respectively reported for the alcoholic.

Rootman and Lafare's 1965 survey is particularly interesting because it was done in a Saskatchewan town very similar to the ones studied by the Cummings. Yet his results show the public's ability to identify mental illness had increased markedly; 95 percent identified the paranoid schizophrenic, 67 percent identified the simple schizophrenic, and 71 percent identified the alcoholic.

Implications

Although the findings of Star in 1950 and the Cummings in 1951 could be considered as support for the hypothesis that the public will avoid seeing evidence of mental illness, the Baltimore study and six other studies since 1960 do not duplicate the earlier findings (table 4). This is true whether the area studied is urban, such as New York or Baltimore; rural, as in Kentucky, Easton, or Carroll County; or even in a Canadian town similar to that studied by the Cummings.

All the surveys have found large majorities of the respondents able to identify the Star case description of a paranoid schizophrenic as indicative of mental illness, with the percentages after 1960 exceeding 89 percent. At least two-thirds of those interviewed in the six post-1960 studies using the Star vignette of a simple schizophrenic were able to identify it as indicative of mental illness. Only one of the later studies found less than 62 percent of its respondents able to identify the Star case description of an alcoholic as indicative of mental illness, and that one still reported substantially more identification than either Star or the Cummings.

We analyzed the results of our Baltimore study for a wide variety of variables. Age, sex, education, social class, family income, type of birthplace, and previous contact with the mentally ill were all significantly correlated with identification of the vignettes. However, no subgroup of these variables which included more than 2 percent of the total respondents had less than 75 percent of the group able to identify two or more of the case descriptions. The only important groups not well represented were social classes I and II (Hollingshead 1957)—a small percentage of the total population—where only 60 percent identified two or more vignettes as indicative of mental illness. Therefore no reasonable sample bias could explain away the results.

The possibility that "yea-saying" (Couch and Kenniston 1960) had influenced the findings was examined in our Baltimore study and Dohrenwend's 1964 survey (Dohrenwend and Chin-Shong 1967). It was found to be minimal in both.

The data obtained from every study in recent years have failed to indicate any public inability or unwillingness to identify mental illness. It must therefore be concluded that the public recognizes evidence of mental illness when it is presented.

The fact that the public recognizes mental illness may or may not be of significance for mental health programming. What is significant is the way the assumption that the public does not recognize mental illness has been used as an explanation for underutilization of services and has been used to attack medical models of emotional disturbance and to support a theory which equates psychological disturbance with social deviancy. The documented capacity of the public to recognize mental illness should lead to reexamination of these beliefs.

CHAPTER 4

Contact with the Mentally Ill

If mental illness carries such stigma, if shame is felt if someone close is mentally ill, one hardly would expect widespread public acknowledgment that friends and relatives have been mentally ill. What people are ashamed of they hide, and so it is important to find out whether people hide contact with the mentally ill. This area concerns what people say, rather than what they do or think; thus the survey technique is an ideal method of investigation.

Methodology

We explored the idea of contact in three ways. First, both groups of respondents were asked various questions about the degree of contact with former mental hospital patients. Secondly, in the UAW survey the degree of contact with individuals who had been otherwise connected with psychiatric treatment or problems was investigated. These are direct tests of the hypothesis, and both the admission of contact and its closeness are examined. Thirdly, the UAW study examined the willingness of psychiatric patients to admit the fact of their treatment.

Although the Cummings have held that a former mental hospital patient must consider himself stigmatized (1965, p. 136), it does not necessarily follow that he would willingly expose himself to stigmatization by freely disclosing his psychiatric history. Thus, it will also be likely that if there is a strong public denial of contact with the mentally ill, a psychiatric patient will not admit his history in an interview situation.

As detailed in Appendix D, 79 union members known to be psychiatric patients were added to the UAW study's sample consisting of 888 other union members. The interviewers were in no way identified as part of a psychiatric survey or associated with the Department of Psychiatry or Johns Hopkins Hospital, although in a few cases they did use an endorsement from the Johns Hopkins School of Public Health and Hygiene to avoid refusals.

The interviewers knew that the study would "probably" uncover some patients in treatment, but known patients were not identified or distinguished from the general sample. However, during debriefing many interviewers indicated an awareness that psychiatric patients had been purposely placed in the study.

Findings

We found that 63 percent of the Baltimore respondents and 59 percent of the UAW sample admitted knowing someone who had been hospitalized for mental illness (tables 5 and 6). Also, 26 percent of the UAW respondents admitted knowing someone who had seen a psychiatrist even though they had not known anyone who had been hospitalized, making a total of 85 percent of that study who stated that they knew at least one person who either had been hospitalized for mental illness or had seen a psychiatrist. An additional 2 percent of the total UAW population surveyed claimed to know someone with an untreated mental illness, while 3 percent had themselves talked to a doctor about nervous or mental problems in their own families.

Eighty-four percent of the known psychiatric patients stated that they had seen a psychiatrist, while 16 percent denied such consultation. However, more than half (9 percent) of

TABLE 5. Percentage of Baltimore Sample Admitting Contact with Individuals Hospitalized for Mental Illness

Have you ever known anyone hospitalized for mental illness?

Response	
No	37%
Yes	63
Total	100%

Who was that?

Closest Relationship Admitted	
Self	1%
Immediate family	9
Other relative	12
Close friend	14
Acquaintance	25
Other	2
Total	63%

NOTE: N = 1,738.

the deniers were being treated by other types of mental health professionals. With or without these 9 percent, an overwhelming majority of the known psychiatric patients did not deny their treatment. Similarly, when the UAW members were asked several questions about their personal experiences with psychiatric treatment, 35 percent stated that they had sought some type of help, with 2 percent affirming that they had been patients in a mental hospital.

Implications

The data from the UAW study showing little denial of contact with the mentally ill might be questioned because of the sample's narrow demographic base, common union membership, and residential propinquity. However, the Baltimore

TABLE 6. Percentage of UAW Sample Admitting Contact with Individuals Hospitalized for Mental Illness (Wave I)

Have you ever known anyone hospitalized for mental illness?

Response	
No	41%
Yes	59
Total	100%

Who was that?

Closest Relationship Admitted	
Self	2%
Spouse	1
Relative	23
Close friend	11
Acquaintance	22
Total	59%

NOTE: N = 888.

survey, without these limitations, yielded very similar results. Also, Elinson, Padilla, and Perkins (1967) reported that "one out of two" New York City adults claimed to have known someone who had received help for mental and emotional problems, with Edgerton and Bentz (1969) finding a similar figure for rural North Carolina.

A wish to deny contact with the mentally ill might also cause an individual to report his relationship to the mentally ill as more distant than it really was. However, a majority of the reported contacts are assigned to family and close friends rather than to mere acquaintances (tables 5 and 6). That 26 percent of the UAW respondents reported that either they or some relative of theirs had been hospitalized for mental illness is not the result of an abnormal rate of mental disorder. We did a detailed study of this population using the MacMillan

TABLE 7. Comparison of Responses on Concealing Mental Illness (1950–1960)

Place	Date	N	Percentage of Yes Responses to "If a family member became mentally ill, I would tell friends."
Louisville[a]	1950	3,971	44%
New Jersey[b]	1954	1,209	66
Austin[c]	1954	355	62
Purdue #56[d]	1959	2,000	60
Four Texas communities[e]	1958–59	591	71

a. Woodward 1951.
b. Audience Research, Inc. 1954a.
c. Jaco 1957a.
d. Purdue University 1959.
e. Crawford, Rollins, and Sutherland 1960.

Index and found symptom levels comparable to or less than other populations (MacMillan 1957; Spiro, Siassi, and Crocetti 1972).

On the other hand, if the hypothesis of contact denial were valid, there would be relatively few reports of family members' hospitalization. A number of studies have asked respondents whether or not they would tell their friends if a family member became ill (table 7). Only Woodward's 1951 study found less than 60 percent of those questioned willing to tell their friends of a relative's mental illness.

Yarrow, Clausen, and Robbins (1955, p. 34) found a "predominant" expectation of stigma in their study of thirty-three wives of mental hospital patients, but Freeman and Simmons concluded, after interviewing 702 relatives of former mental patients, that a feeling of stigma was characteristic of "only a minority" (1961, p. 321). Part of this difference may result from the former study being about currently hospitalized patients and the latter about discharged patients.

Summary and Conclusions

Fifty-nine percent and 63 percent of the UAW and Baltimore respondents respectively reported knowing someone who had been hospitalized for mental illness. In the UAW survey, an additional 26 percent of those interviewed reported knowing someone who had consulted a psychiatrist. A majority of the reported contacts were with relatives or close friends.

Four of five other studies have reported a substantial majority of respondents as willing to inform their friends of a relative's mental illness (table 7). The more recent and extensive of two studies of the relatives of mental hospital patients also finds a small minority who report feeling stigmatized. A subsidiary UAW study of persons known to be receiving psychiatric care found that 84 percent freely admitted their treatment.

The hypothesis that the public will deny contact with the mentally ill refers to the ratio between those who admit having such contact and those who have actually had it. However, even if 100 percent of the respondents had, in fact, some contact with the mentally ill, it seems that an overwhelming majority are not reluctant to admit such contact.

CHAPTER 5

Negative Stereotypes

The belief that the public harbors rigid negative stereotypes of mentally ill individuals is central to the idea that psychopathological behavior is simply a form of social deviance. Further it suggests that because negative stereotypes fill a strong psychological need for predictability of social behavior, these attitudes are extremely refractory to change (Cumming and Cumming 1957). Therefore, establishing the existence or nonexistence of these attitudes is important in understanding the role of the mentally ill in our society. For example, are the mentally ill regarded as entitled to the sick role or any other exculpatory role or are they regarded as legitimate objects of punishment?

Negative stereotypes and hostile attitudes can be directly measured. One may ask such questions as whether people consider the mentally ill criminal and dangerous and whether they should be kept behind locked doors.

If the public does not accord the mentally ill the sick role, then a majority of the population should not agree that mental illness is an illness like any other, nor should they recommend medical treatment for psychiatric symptoms. Furthermore, if the public has a strong negatively stereotyped attitude toward the mentally ill, then a majority of the population should see mental illness as a basically homogeneous category. Similarly the mentally ill should probably be regarded as incurable. Finally, if the public sees the mentally ill as social deviants who threaten society and are thus subject to social sanctions, then the majority of the population should consider almost all mentally ill persons dangerous or criminal and should see mental hospitals as prisons. Thus most people should want the mentally ill "put away" and should oppose modalities of care that retain the mentally ill in the community. All of these suppositions are investigated in this chapter.

Findings

We found that a large majority of the respondents in both the UAW and Baltimore surveys see mental illness as similar to other illnesses. Ninety-eight percent of the UAW respondents agreed that the mentally ill require a doctor's care just as much as people with any other illness. In the Baltimore study, after each Star case description was read (see chapter 3 for texts), everyone was asked whether or not the described person should see a doctor. Medical care was recommended for the paranoid and simple schizophrenic by 95 percent and 93 percent of those interviewed, and for the alcoholic by 84 percent.

When asked whether the cases described in the Star vignettes were curable, 79 percent of the Baltimore respondents thought the paranoid schizophrenic could be cured, 72 percent thought the same for the simple schizophrenic, and 57 percent, for the alcoholic. Eighty-nine percent of those interviewed in the UAW study said that most mentally ill people could be cured with proper treatment.

The Baltimore respondents gave a very high percentage of "enlightened" or professionally acceptable responses to a variety of statements about the nature and treatment of mental illness (table 8). One of the statements most thoroughly studied by the Baltimore survey was the public's attitude toward home care for the mentally ill. The general acceptability of this idea is shown in table 9.

Another series of questions was based on case descriptions of a severely depressed young girl, an involutional depressed male breadwinner, and an elderly senile woman (texts are in Appendix A). In each case the respondents were told that the doctor had offered the alternatives of hospitalization or psychiatric services in the home, with each having the same

TABLE 8. Percentage of Baltimore Sample Giving "Enlightened" Responses About the Nature and Treatment of Mental Illness

Statement	Response	Percentage
There are many different types of mental illness.	Agree	92%
All people with the same mental illness act the same way.	Disagree	83
Everyone who has a mental illness should be placed in a mental hospital.	Disagree	57
Almost all persons who have a mental illness are dangerous.	Disagree	74
The best way to handle people in mental hospitals is to keep them behind locked doors.	Disagree	77
Every mental hospital should be surrounded by a high fence and guards.	Disagree	62
People who have been in a state mental hospital are no more likely to commit crimes than people who have never been in a state mental hospital.	Agree	59

NOTE: N = 1,738.

TABLE 9. Percentage of Baltimore Respondents Giving Favorable Responses to Statements About Home Care for the Mentally Ill

Statement	Response	Percentage
If someone living in the same family with me became mentally ill, I would certainly try to take care of them at home if the doctor thought it wouldn't do any harm.	Agree	83%
Sometimes it is better for a person with a mental illness to live with his or her family instead of being in a mental hospital.	Agree	74
People who have *some* kinds of mental illness can be taken care of at home.	Agree	84

NOTE: N = 1,738.

TABLE 10. Percentage of Respondents Recommending Home Care or Hospitalization for Described Cases of Mental Illness, by Recommendation (Baltimore, 1960)

Case Description	Recommendations of Respondents: Hospitalization	Home Care	Depends	Don't Know and No Answer	Total
Severely depressed young girl	40%	56%	2%	2%	100%
Involutional depressed male breadwinner	49	46	3	2	100
Elderly senile woman	41	50	5	4	100

NOTE: N = 1,738.

TABLE 11. Reasons Given by Baltimore Respondents for Recommending Home Care for Three Described Cases of Mental Illness (N = 1,738)

Reason	Type of Case: Depression	Involutional Depression	Senility
Patient needs tender loving care	44%	41%	35%
Change of environment bad for patient	27	32	25
Mental hospitals have bad effect	24	12	4
Not really mentally ill	24	29	54
Try home first, hospital last resort	16	21	13
Mental hospitals are inadequate	12	6	5
Hospital makes patient feel neglected	9	5	4
Stigma attached to hospitalization	6	5	1
Moral obligation to keep home	5	3	25
Miscellaneous	10	11	9
Don't know	1	1	1
Total	100%	100%	100%

NOTE: Percentages actually add to more than 100 percent because some respondents gave more than one answer.

prognosis and cost. Table 10 indicates that home care is more recommended than not. Half of those interviewed advised home care in two or more cases, and only 19 percent never favored it.

Probing revealed a wide variety of reasons for the recommendations that were made. Tables 11 and 12 detail the reasons given and their frequency. Some respondents gave more than

TABLE 12. Reasons Given by Baltimore Respondents for Recommending Hospitalization for Three Described Cases of Mental Illness (N = 1,738)

Reason	Type of Case: Depression	Involutional Depression	Senility
Hospital provides better quality care than possible at home	78%	55%	46%
Change in environment helpful	42	42	27
Hospital provides greater quantity of care than possible at home	30	17	14
Violence and custodial care handled better in hospital	9	13	28
Nursing care required too much for family	1	26	20
Family will suffer because of presence of patient	2	27	43
Total	100%	100%	100%

NOTE: Percentages add to more than 100 percent because some respondents gave more than one answer.

one reason. The main import of these tables is that the reasons most commonly given for urging either plan were rational, patient-centered ones. They did not seem to reflect a desire simply to get the mentally ill out of the way. Punitive attitudes are noticeable only by their absence. The stigma of hospitalization is not considered an important factor in urging home treatment.

Implications

The Joint Commission on Mental Illness and Health, which largely subscribed to the "theory of rejection," argued that "the principle of sameness applied to the mentally sick versus the physically sick . . . has become a cardinal tenet of mental health education. But this principle has largely fallen on deaf ears" (1961, p. 59). Our findings from the Baltimore and UAW studies seem to indicate otherwise. A great majority of the respondents find medical treatment appropriate for mental illness in general and for the specific cases described in the Star vignettes. The work of Edgerton and Bentz is in accord with ours as they report that a majority of their respondents in two rural North Carolina counties "share the view that 'mental illness is the most serious health problem in this country' . . . and that 'mental illness is an illness like any other'" (1969, p. 474). Elinson, Padilla, and Perkins report 69 percent of the New York City sample agreeing with the latter statement (1967, p. 19).

The joint commission claimed that there was a "pervasive defeatism" (1961, p. xix) about the mentally ill. On the contrary we found the public to be quite optimistic about a mentally ill person's prognosis. Edgerton and Bentz's findings were similar. They reported that 75 percent or more of their respondents disagreed with the statements that "not much can be done for mental illness," "once a person has been mentally ill, he can never be normal and healthy again," "little can be done for patients in a mental hospital," and "few people who enter mental hospitals ever leave." Sixty-five percent of those interviewed felt that "most mental patients will make a good adjustment to the community on release from the hospital" (1969, pp. 474–75).

The New York City study by Elinson, Padilla, and Perkins found 80 percent or more of those interviewed disagreeing with the statements that "to become a patient in a mental hospital is to become a failure for life" and "not much can be done for mental illness" (1967, p. 124). They also noted that "belief in . . . the recovery from mental illness may be inferred from the disagreement by two persons in three (67% with the statement that 'it is easy to recognize someone who once had a serious mental illness')" (p. 19). They also reported that 77 percent of their respondents felt that the chances of a mental patient's "getting better" were fair to excellent (p. 130).

These data do not permit any conclusions about the public's feelings on the curability of mental illness relative to that of other diseases. Rather, the import of the data seems to be that the public considers mental illness largely curable. Evidently Star at one point in her study had similar findings, for the joint commission quotes her as saying "the average American adult knows that mental illness can be treated and knows that its treatment involves special facilities—psychiatrists and institutions" (1961, p. 76). However, the joint commission goes on to say that "Star drew a sharp contrast between these findings and data in another part of her survey" (p. 76). The contrasted data were her findings that only the paranoid schizophrenic vignette was identified as mentally ill by a majority of the public. This permitted the joint commission to conclude that there is "a kind of lip-service being paid to mental health information to the effect that psychotics *are* sick and *are* treatable, but behind this [is] a rejecting attitude toward patients and towards treatment" (p. 76). Since the data presented in chapter 3 seem to indicate that the public is currently able to identify mental illness, Star's work now allows the conclusion that the mentally ill are not seen as incurable.

The joint commission notes that "the popular stereotype of the 'raving madman' as the only kind of person who goes to mental hospitals needs to be dispelled" (1961, p. xix). Throughout much of the joint commission's report there seems to be an assumption that the public sees only one type of mentally ill person and that one is "wild" and "out of control"

(p. xix). Quoting Star, the joint commission writes: "The neurotic is looked upon with moral disapproval; the psychotic *as dangerous*" (emphasis added, p. 77). Since it had already been stated that the public recognizes only the extreme psychotic as mentally ill, it is a fair assumption that these are the characteristics the joint commission sees the public attributing to all the mentally ill. In another section the commission draws the analogy it thinks the public makes between illness and criminality: "Since the beginning of history . . . society has pursued what we now regard as a superstitious and retaliatory approach in the care of the mentally ill. The instrument of this approach is punishment, pursuant to the theory [that] . . . either sinful or *criminal* behavior calls for punishment" (emphasis added, p. 25).

Some of the statements in the Baltimore study were designed to test the public's perceptions of mental illness as a homogeneous category and of the mentally ill as criminal, dangerous, or fear-provoking. Table 13 presents a composite of the Baltimore study and six other surveys that made some of the same statements. The results obtained by the six studies are strikingly consistent in seeming to oppose the idea that the public views the mentally ill in a condemnatory manner.

The question of whether or not the mentally ill are seen as dangerous or criminally deviant is closely related to the nature of the public's perception of mental hospitalization. As noted above in this chapter and in chapter 2, the "theory of rejection" leads to the idea that the public has a need to put the mentally ill away. The theory also implies that the public sees mental hospitals as places of punishment or confinement similar to prisons.

However, the overwhelming disagreement with two of the statements in table 13—that mental hospitals should be locked, fenced, and guarded—does not indicate the widespread existence of such conceptions of mental hospitalization. Elinson, Padilla, and Perkins also explored this question by asking their sample which of several other institutions a state mental

TABLE 13. Percentage of Respondents in Various Studies Giving "Enlightened" Responses About the Nature and Treatment of Mental Illness, by Place of Study

Statement	Response	Purdue #56[a] 1959 (N = 2,000)	Baltimore 1960 (N = 1,738)	Carroll Co., Md.[b] 1961 (N = 139)	Easton, Md.[c] 1962 (N = 100)	Kentucky[d] 1963 (N = 970)	Regina, Canada[e] 1965 (N = 102)	Rural N.C.[f] 1969 (N = 960)
There are many different kinds of mental illness.	Agree	—	92%	95%	94%	91%	90%	96%
All people with the same mental illness act the same way.	Disagree	—	83	90	83	83	85	80
Everyone who has a mental illness should be placed in a mental hospital.	Disagree	—	57	—	—	59	—	—
Almost all persons who have a mental illness are dangerous.	Disagree	—	74	—	—	76	83	—

The best way to handle people in a mental hospital is to keep them behind locked doors.	Disagree	—	77	78	84	78	87	—
Every mental hospital should be surrounded by a high fence and guards.	Disagree	72%	62	61	78	61	78	51
People who have been in a state (provincial) mental hospital are no more likely to commit crimes than people who have never been in a state (provincial) hospital.	Agree	71	59	73	57	65	50	—

a. Purdue University 1959.
b. M. Lemkau 1962.
c. Meyer 1964.
d. Kentucky Mental Health Planning Commission 1964.
e. Rootman and Lafare 1965.
f. Edgerton and Bentz 1969.

TABLE 14. Similarity Between State Mental Hospitals and Other Institutions Seen by a New York City Sample

A state mental hospital is most like a:	
General hospital	33%
TB sanitarium	15
Prison	23
Boarding house	2
Nursing home	15
Don't know or no answer	12
Total	100%

SOURCE: Ellinson, Padilla, and Perkins 1967.
NOTE: N = 2,610.

hospital most resembled (table 14). Their finding that only 23 percent likened a mental hospital to a prison seems to be in line with the data noted in table 13.

In the same study 83 percent of the respondents agreed with the statement that "even if most patients do not get better there, state mental hospitals are needed because they do a job of protecting the community" (1967, p. 125). As the authors pointed out, this could support the idea that the public sees the mentally ill as dangerous and the mental hospital as primarily a place to keep them out of the way (p. xv). However, 54 percent of the identical group disagreed with the explicit statement that "it is necessary to use mental hospitals for keeping people out of the way" (p. 218). Since 63 percent of them had also found state mental hospitals to be most like other medical facilities, it is possible that they read the first quoted statement in this paragraph to mean something other than that the job of mental hospitals is to protect the community. They might, for example, have interpreted the question as asking whether or not state mental hospitals are needed even if most of the patients do not get better there.

It could be argued that if the public preferred hospitalization of the mentally ill, that response would support the conclusion that the public wishes to put the mentally ill away, out of sight. The validity of such an argument depends on the public's knowledge of other forms of treatment. If hospitalization is all it knows, the choice does not necessarily imply a desire to be rid of the mentally ill.

Edgerton and Bentz wrote that in North Carolina, "in recent years, the idea of a comprehensive mental health center operating in the local community has been promulgated as the preferred method for meeting the mental health needs of the community. We were interested in determining the extent to which the communities were aware of this new concept. Less than 1% of our sample had ever heard of the idea; and these few respondents had an understanding of the mental health center that was superficial, at best" (1969, pp. 472–73).

In New York City, Elinson, Padilla, and Perkins found that more than a third of their sample could not correctly name any general hospital in the city that had beds for mental patients, while three-fourths could not correctly name any mental health clinic (1967, p. 10). It would seem easy to overestimate the public's actual knowledge of alternatives to state mental hospitals.

We found that, as detailed in tables 10, 11, and 12, 81 percent of the Baltimore respondents recommended home care for at least one of the three cases described to them. A majority of the reasons given for advising both home care and hospitalization were concerned with the quality and quantity of patient care rather than with any feeling of rejection. This result is similar to that reported in the New York City survey where respondents were given brief descriptions of fourteen types of community-based health services and programs. All of the services except foster care were urged for use with the mentally ill in New York City by a majority of those interviewed (Elinson, Padilla, and Perkins 1967, p. 142). The most popular was neighborhood aftercare and rehabilitation which was favored by 91 percent. Of the other care-providing services, psychiatric service in a general hospital was approved by 89 percent of the respondents; halfway houses, by 85 percent; home treat-

TABLE 15. Percentages in Five Studies Giving Favorable Responses to Statements About Home Care for the Mentally Ill

Statement	Response	Baltimore[a] 1960 (N = 1,738)	Carroll Co., Md.[b] 1961 (N = 139)	Easton, Md.[c] 1962 (N = 100)	Kentucky[d] 1964 (N = 970)	Saskatchewan, Canada[e] 1965 (N = 102)
People who have *some* kinds of mental illness can be taken care of at home.	Agree	84%	88%	89%	85%	74%
If someone living in the same family with me became mentally ill, I would certainly try to take care of them at home *if* the doctor thought it wouldn't do any harm.	Agree	83	98	87	79	77
Sometimes it is better for a person with a mental illness to live with his or her family instead of being in a mental hospital.	Agree	74	—	81	89	71

a. Crocetti and Lemkau 1963
b. M. Lemkau 1962
c. Meyer 1964
d. Kentucky Mental Health Planning Commission 1964
e. Rootman and Lafare 1965

ment by psychiatrists, by 78 percent; and open mental hospitals, by 63 percent (Elinson, Padilla and Perkins 1967, p. 142). Table 15 shows the generally favorable responses to statements about home care made in five studies, including the Baltimore survey.

Summary and Conclusions

The "theory of rejection" is predicated on the idea that the public has a stereotyped and undifferentiated view of mental illness and the mentally ill. It also depends on the argument that the mentally ill are seen as socially deviant and therefore as dangerous, criminal, fear-provoking, essentially incurable, and not ill in the same way as those with physical illnesses. The public is accordingly supposed to want the mentally ill to be put away from sight, to see mental hospitals as prisons, and to be opposed to home care.

However, an overwhelming majority of those interviewed in our surveys and six other studies done since 1960 felt that there were many different types of mental illness and that behavior patterns varied even within a given mental illness (table 13). Our data also show that the public believes that mental illness is curable, with 89 percent agreeing with that general statement and from 57 percent to 70 percent considering the Star cases curable. Similar results were found by Elinson, Padilla, and Perkins (1967, p. 130).

Although Star found the mentally ill regarded as dangerous, studies since 1960 have uniformly reported three-quarters or more of their respondents denying the statement that almost all mentally ill persons are dangerous (table 13). The Cummings have argued that the public responds to the mentally ill with a "pattern of denial, isolation, and insulation." The second step of "isolation of the affected person in a mental hospital [occurs] when mental illness can no longer be denied" (1957, p. 99). Thus the public should very greatly prefer hospitalization to other forms of treatment of the mentally ill, especially home care, and do so with the purpose of having them out of the way.

However, data from the Baltimore survey and four other studies show that from 71 percent to 89 percent of those interviewed accept home care for some of the mentally ill, with from 77 percent to 98 percent being "certainly" willing to attempt home care of a mentally ill family member if the doctor approved (table 15). The Baltimore survey also found from 46 percent to 56 percent of the respondents favoring home care over hospitalization where cost and prognosis were the same (table 10). The stated reasons for both choices appeared to reflect a concern for the patient's welfare rather than a wish to put him away (tables 11 and 12). This acceptance of home care for the mentally ill is all the more remarkable in the light of the public's ignorance of alternatives to hospitalization (Edgerton and Bentz 1969, pp. 472-73).

It thus seems that the strong consensus of the current data is not in agreement with the idea that the public has a stereotyped conception of mental illness or that the mentally ill are seen as dangerous criminals to be properly put away in prisonlike mental hospitals. Rather, the data suggest the public's awareness of different types of mental illness, the public's desire that mental hospitals be facilities for treatment, and the public's willingness to regard home care or hospital care for the mentally ill in the same light as for any other illness.

CHAPTER 6

Social Distance

Prejudice manifests itself in social barriers and social distance. Surveys using social-distance questions have invariably reflected the barriers erected by a society against the members of groups held in extreme prejudice. Social-distance scales have been used to measure the extent to which a society rejects social intimacy with the members of a given group. The presence or absence of expressed social distance from the mentally ill must therefore have a strong role in shaping our definition of how the mentally ill are seen in our society. Without proof of social distance, assertions that mentally ill persons face severe prejudice must be viewed as having no substance.

While the concept of social distance is reasonably well defined, empirical methods of measuring it are not very precise and well determined. The next three chapters are devoted to an examination of the concept of social distance and its related factors in terms of the general public and the mentally ill. This chapter will briefly explore the history of the concept of social distance and its measurement as a foundation for presenting the overall findings of the present studies and their comparison with the results of other surveys. Chapter 7 will investigate the correlation of social distance with the attitudinal factors already discussed in chapters 3, 4, and 5. Chapter 8 will discuss some of the inferences that may be drawn from such analysis.

The Measurement of Social Distance

The concept of social distance has been used in many different fields. Although it is applicable to all social relationships, social distance is often seen as fundamentally related to class and family structure. Murdock (1949), in his volume on cross-cultural comparisons, states:

> When a society is stratified into social classes or castes the cultural differences and "social distance" ordinarily characteristic of geographically separated groups are commonly manifested by groups that are only socially and hierarchically distinct. Endogamous preferences thus become associated with caste and class strata. (p. 265)

In the same text he writes: "As it affects sex and marriage preferences, ethnocentrism establishes a negative gradient of ethnic endogamy which operates with increasing force in proportion to social distance, i.e., in relation to the diminution of social ties and the multiplication of cultural differences" (p. 315). In a footnote he credits Bogardus as the source of "this apt term."

Although Bogardus was the first to systematically measure social distance (1925), the lack of correlation between physical proximity and social intimacy has often been noted in literature and history. Writing about the colonial American, Crèvecoeur observed that in the thinly settled backwoods, "the forces of leveling are strongest, it is there that the last remnants of old world distinctions and privileges are swept away" (Parrington 1930) or, in other words, physical distance but social proximity. Conversely the physical proximity but social distance between southern slaves and their owners has also been described frequently.

Murdock was primarily concerned with ethnic groups, but his statement offers one operational definition of social distance, namely, the concurrent diminution of social contacts and multiplication of perceived differences between mutually defined social groups. In terms of social consequences it does not matter whether the diminution of social contact or the multiplication of perceived differences is antecedent. In either event, the outcome is the same. With greater social distance, fewer social relationships will occur between the two groups. For instance, social distance plays a significant role in defining who may be married to whom within any social system, irrespective of physical proximity. Through this effect the concept of social distance becomes linked to a much more extensive body of psychological and anthropological theories. Bogardus, though primarily concerned with ethnic groups, attempted to establish a social-distance scale for determining the degree of rejection or acceptance of any particular group. A partial example of his original scale is reproduced below.

Directions: According to my first feeling reactions I would willingly admit members of each race (as a class, and not the best I have known, nor the worst members) to one or more of the classifications which I have marked.

	Canadians	Chinese	English	French	Germans	Hindus
To close kinship by marriage						
To my club as personal chums						
To my street as neighbors						
To employment in my occupation in my country						
To citizenship in my country						
As visitors only to my country						
Would exclude from my country						

"Although Bogardus' data did not show his scale to be scalar in measurement there did seem to be a progression, at least for a large sample. Mathematically more precise methods such

TABLE 16. A Comparison of Social Distance Between Various Ethnic Groups

Would Admit to:	Negroes	German Jews	Germans
Close kinship by marriage	1%	8%	54%
My street as neighbors	12	25	78
Employment in my occupation	39	40	83
Citizenship in my country	57	54	87

SOURCE: Bogardus 1928.
NOTE: N = 1,725.

as Thurstone's paired comparisons have resulted in relative degrees of preference for social groups which are almost identical with those reported by Bogardus" (Murphy, Murphy, and Newcomb 1937, p. 898).

Table 16 shows some of Bogardus's findings concerning the social distance expressed by a white native-born American population of mid-1920 toward several ethnic groups. It is included in order to provide perspective on the social-distance data reported concerning former mental patients.

Social Distance and the Mentally Ill

In the present studies, like many others, scales patterned after Bogardus's were used to investigate the social distance that the public places between itself and the mentally ill. We considered that a test of the relationship between possession of the characteristics of being or having been mentally ill and acceptability in social relationships was a test of the hypothesis that the public will reject social intimacy with the mentally ill.

The results of the scales used in both the Baltimore and UAW studies are shown in tables 17 and 18. The UAW surveys divided the responses into finer categories. When the results

TABLE 17. Responses of Baltimore Sample to Four Social-Distance Statements

Statement	Agree	Disagree	Don't Know
I wouldn't hesitate to work with someone who had been mentally ill.	81%	17%	2%
I would be willing to room with someone who had been a patient in a mental hospital.	50	45	5
I can imagine myself falling in love with a person who had been mentally ill.	51	44	5
We should strongly discourage our children from marrying anyone who has been mentally ill.	49	46	5

NOTE: N = 1,737

of the UAW study's first wave are analyzed as a scale, 85 percent of the respondents fit the scalar pattern. Only 4 percent of those interviewed are totally rejecting of any relationship with the mentally ill, while 58 percent are accepting of all relationships.

The second wave of the UAW study did not use exactly the same questions as the first. Two additional questions were asked, and instead of only describing the hypothetical person as having a history of mental illness, some more, generally favorable, information was given. Also some of the people described were not identified as mentally ill at all. The reasons for these differences and a discussion of the resulting data are given in chapter 8. Here we have combined all of the different descriptions of the hypothetical person which mentioned a history of mental hospitalization. There was virtually unanimous acceptance of former mental hospital patients as neighbors, fellow club members, and co-workers, while 85 percent of the respondents were willing to room with such

TABLE 18. Responses of UAW Workers to Three Social-Distance Questions (Wave I)

Question	Definitely Willing	Probably Willing	Probably Unwilling	Definitely Unwilling	Don't Know	Total
How would you feel about working on the same job with someone who had been mentally ill?	49%	45%	3%	2%	1%	100%
How would you feel about rooming with someone who had been mentally ill?	14	50	18	15	3	100
Could you imagine yourself falling in love with someone who had been mentally ill?	15	49	14	13	9	100

NOTE: N = 888.

a person and 78 percent would not discourage their children from marrying him (table 19).

Since there was no appreciable reluctance by the respondents of the UAW second wave to having a former mental hospital patient as a neighbor, fellow club member, or co-worker, we will only analyze the answers concerning willingness to "rent a room in your home to" or "have one of your children marry" such a person. (The use of the terms *willing* and *willingness* without qualification indicates that those who responded with "definitely willing" and "probably willing" have been summed; *unwilling* when unqualified means the summation of those "unwilling" and "probably unwilling.") Analysis by

TABLE 19. Answers of 579 UAW Respondents to Five Social-Distance Questions (Wave II)

Question	Total	Definitely Willing	Probably Willing	Probably Unwilling	Definitely Unwilling	Don't Know and No answer
Have as a neighbor?	100%	66%	33%	—[a]	1%	—[a]
Have as member of favorite club?	100	67	31	1%	1	—[a]
Work with?	100	69	29	1	1	—[a]
Rent room in home to?	100	38	47	7	7	1%
Have child marry?	100	27	51	7	7	8

NOTE: Seventy-four respondents answering to "normal" description excluded.
a. Less than 1 percent.

the variables discussed here, where comparable, did not significantly differ from that of the first wave.

We found no significant differences between the sex of the respondent and his or her attitude toward renting a room to or marrying a former mental hospital patient. However, when the "willing" category is broken down, the women are more conditional in their answers. The difference for the "rent room to" answer is not too far from significant ($p < .10$) and that for "children marry" is definitely significant ($p < .005$). Neither did we find a significant relationship between income and willingness to rent a room to a former mental hospital patient. However, the group with an income of less than $7,500 a year is significantly less willing to have one of its children marry such a person ($p < .025$), although even in this group 67 percent are so willing.

Education was quite concentrated in this sample. Only 4 percent of the respondents had more than twelve years of schooling, while 1 percent had less than four years. The remainder were approximately evenly divided between the categories of four to eight years, nine to eleven, and twelve years of education. This limits the possibilities for significant differences, and none were found. There was, however, a slight tendency for the least educated to be less accepting of the mentally ill.

Our analysis of the relationship between age and the social-distance questions showed no significant difference for the "rent room to" question. However with age a steadily lessening acceptance of the former mental hospital patient was noted for the other questions. This trend is much more evident in the "have one of your children marry" question where the differences between all groups are extremely significant ($p < .001$). This is comprised of two significant age breaks, under forty versus over forty and from forty-one to fifty versus over fifty. These differences are primarily between the "probably willing" and "unwilling" categories, with the "definitely unwilling" in the over-forty group being nearly three times that of the under-thirty respondents.

As described in chapter 4, a variety of questions was asked about the respondent's contact with people who either had been patients in a mental hospital or had consulted a psychiatrist. By considering only the closest relative and the most intensive level of care, the investigators obtained an unduplicated count. Of all the possible combinations and permutations in the two questions of the four levels of contact and the two different ways of considering the acceptance, only two are significant. More respondents who had had some contact with the mentally ill were definitely willing to rent a room to a former mental hospital patient than those who had had no contact at all ($p < .05$). This was especially true of the respondents whose contact with the mentally ill had been through an acquaintance ($p < .01$).

The inexact definition of contact and the lack of information as to its emotional significance to the respondent make it difficult to interpret this finding's positive implications. It does seem, however, opposite to the joint commission's claim that "the mentally ill . . . disturb and repel others" (1961, p. xviii). Contact with the mentally ill seems to be largely unrelated to social acceptance of former mental hospital patients.

Implications

Although final interpretation of any scaled data depends on the establishment of a base line (see chapter 8), the "raw" findings of these three studies are not without meaning. The clear distinction found between the most intimate social and physical relationships and the others is reminiscent of that found by Bogardus in table 16.

Perhaps the most striking finding is that the mentally ill need not fear rejection in any of the most common social interactions, such as employment, housing, and social clubs. Even in the most intimate circumstances, they could expect rejection less than half the time. This level of social distance is comparable to, or better than, that encountered by a German in the 1920s, and of an entirely different intensity from that experienced by a Negro or a Jew at that time (Bogardus 1928). A person with a history of mental illness is more welcome as a suitor now than a Negro or a Jew was as a citizen in 1925.

In sum, the data in no way support any hypothesis of rejection for the mentally ill in everyday relationships. Nor do they support the hypothesis that the social distance the public feels toward the mentally ill is at all comparable to the classic prejudiced rejection once encountered by various minorities.

The issue of the wording of questions is a vital one in the repetition and comparison of social-distance data obtained from population surveys. A comparison with the results from the two waves of the UAW study may help to clarify this. The second wave used the same sample as the first but after an interval of eighteen months. In one part of the resurvey three of the social-distance questions concerned the same type of relationship as in the first wave, but were worded somewhat differently as detailed below:

Wave I	*Wave II*
How would you feel about working on the same job with someone who has been mentally ill?	If you knew a person had been mentally ill, that is, had once been in a mental hospital, how would you feel about working on the same job with someone like this?
How would you feel about rooming with someone who had been mentally ill?	Suppose you had a room to rent in your home. Would you . . . rent it to someone like this [someone who had once been in a mental hospital]?
Could you imagine yourself falling in love with someone who had been mentally ill?	How would you feel about having one of your children marry someone like this [someone who had once been in a mental hospital]?

The questions in the second wave are more specific, both in terms of the hypothetical person and the relationship considered. If the respondents' replies are largely the same in both waves, the response to such social-distance questions could be considered stable for slightly different wordings as well as in time. We found some instability of response in the more intimate relationships. Admittedly, the analogy between imagining oneself falling in love with someone who had been mentally ill and agreeing to let one's child marry a former mental hospital patient is not so exact as might be wished. Nevertheless, the basic finding, that of majority acceptance, was not changed.

We also analyzed the relative stability of the original accepting and rejecting responses for the "rooming" and "fall in love with" questions. The accepting response was more stable in both cases. Those who were initially willing to accept relationships with the former mental patients were much more stable in their responses than those who were not. The combination of the greater persistence of the accepting responses with the significantly greater acceptance by those respondents under forty years of age permits the inference that the acceptance of the mentally ill is more likely to increase than decrease in the future.

Table 20 shows the responses to social-distance questions about the mentally ill asked in fourteen population studies from 1950 to 1970 in various places. Some of the questions were slightly different in wording, but covered the same social situations: the admissibility of such comparisons has already been discussed. The questions form a hypothetical social-distance scale similar in scope to Bogardus's early work (1928).

Although the studies represent a wide variety of populations and methodologies, they can certainly be compared in some respects. It seems evident that no study finds very much rejection of the mentally ill in the more formal relationships of community member, co-worker, and neighbor. In the more intimate relationships of rooming with, falling in love with, and being related by marriage, the mentally ill are not so readily accepted. The lowest rate was for a study where the Star vignettes were used as descriptions of the mentally ill (Phillips 1963). A Connecticut housewife's willingness to associate with actively ill psychotics may not be realistically related to a Kentucky farmer's acceptance of someone who *had been* mentally ill.

The habit of reporting only one portion of the answer such as is done in table 20 can mask an important "qualified" or "don't know" response. Table 21 notes that the three studies with the next lowest rates of acceptance of the mentally ill into kinship by marriage all had more "qualified" or "don't

TABLE 20. Acceptance of Former Mentally Ill

Place	Date	N	Acceptance by Respondent as: Member of Community	Work-mate	Neighbor	Roommate	One to Fall in Love With	Related by Marriage
Blackfoot, Canada[a]	1950	540	80%	71%	—	44%	32%	27%
London[b]	1956	—	—	92	89%	—	—	21
Purdue[c]	1959	2,000	75	—	—	—	75	—
Baltimore[d]	1960	1,731	—	81	—	51	51	50
Branford, Conn.[e]	1960	300	—	87	97	40	—	17
Easton, Md.[f]	1962	100	—	75	—	55	44	45
Carroll County, Md.[g]	1962	139	—	—	—	64	—	37
Regina, Saskatchewan[h]	1963	102	—	93	—	78	68	—
Kentucky State[i]	1963	970	—	81	—	54	36	25
Suburban Town, Mich.[j]	1956	222	85	72	—	—	—	—
Edinburgh[k]	1966	446	—	77	64	—	—	21
Richmond, N.C.[l]	1969	960	—	88	—	57	—	44
New York City[m]	1963	1,412	—	73	69	23	—	22
Baltimore (UAW)[n]	1970	888	—	90	—	79	64	—

a. Cumming and Cumming 1957.
b. Belson 1957.
c. Purdue University 1959.
d. Crocetti and Lemkau 1963.
e. Phillips 1964.
f. Meyer 1964.
g. M. Lemkau 1962. Eleven percent don't know.
h. Rootman and Lafare 1965.
i. Kentucky Mental Health Planning Commission 1964.
j. Kramer 1956.
k. MacLean 1969.
l. Edgerton and Bentz 1969.
m. Elinson, Padilla, and Perkins 1967.
n. Crocetti, Spiro, and Siassi 1973.

TABLE 21. Compared Responses on Social-Distance Questions in Four Metropolitan Studies

			Workmate Question			Related by Marriage Question		
Place	N	Date	Yes	No	Don't Know, Qualified, No Answer	Yes	No	Don't Know, Qualified, No Answer
Baltimore	1,731	1960	81%	17%	2%	50%	46%	4%
London	—	1956	92	2	6	21	35	44
Edinburgh	446	1966	77	12	11	21	55	24
New York City	1,412	1963	73	12	15	22	52	26

know" responses than accepting ones. Thus, although the Baltimore findings showed a 50 percent acceptance of kinship by marriage to the mentally ill as opposed to 21 percent or 22 percent reported for London, Edinburgh, and New York, the actual number of rejecting answers was comparable for all four studies. Indeed, the London survey's rejection rate was actually 11 percent lower than the Baltimore study.

A similarly close examination of all the other studies is not possible from the available data. With the exceptions of the Branford study for the reasons cited above and the Kentucky study for which "don't know" tabulations are not available, no study since 1956 has reported a rate of rejection of the mentally ill in the most intimate of relationships that is higher than 55 percent while some have noted acceptance rates of up to 68 percent.

Summary and Conclusions

The findings of the present studies show that the mentally ill enjoy nearly total acceptance in all but the most intimate relationships. An examination of social distance by demographic variables and previous contact with the mentally ill shows that age is strongly negatively correlated with acceptance of the mentally ill. Combined with the further findings that accepting attitudes are more persistent than rejecting ones, this result supports the inference that acceptance of the mentally ill will probably increase rather than decrease as time passes. These results are generally in line with those of all studies since 1956 (table 20) except the Branford survey which actually tested a different situation.

This pattern of no rejection of the mentally ill in formal situations and, since 1956, never more than 55 percent rejection even in the most intimate relationships is not at all consistent with the extreme rejection typically experienced by such minority groups as Negroes and Jews in the 1920s (table 16). As defined by social-distance scales the mentally ill simply are not subject to prejudice even vaguely related to racial prejudice. In fact, neither our study nor other recent studies document the presence of clear prejudice toward those who have been mentally ill. Whether prejudice can be said to exist on grounds of "some" social distance presumes that unprejudiced human beings erect no social distance between themselves and strangers (see chapter 8).

CHAPTER 7

The Structure of Social Response to the Mentally Ill

In chapter 3 the ability of the public to identify mental illness from various vignettes describing mentally ill persons was discussed. In chapter 5 general attitudes toward the mentally ill found in population surveys were reviewed. In chapter 6 evidence showing only limited social distance from the mentally ill was presented. In this chapter the presumed interrelationship among the three components of denial, isolation, and rejection of the mentally ill is tested against the data of the Baltimore study.

In addition to four social-distance statements similar to the social-distance questions discussed in chapter 6, the Baltimore study asked three questions about the identification of mental illness, made fifteen statements requiring responses agreeing with or disagreeing with specific attitudes (hereafter referred to as attitude statements), and asked three other questions concerning home care for three types of mentally ill patients. (For the Baltimore study questionnaire, see Appendix A.) Three analytic tools are used in this chapter: a correlation matrix, a canonical correlation, and a factor analysis.

The Correlation Matrix

Table 22 shows the result of a correlation matrix of "enlightened" or "correct" responses to twenty-one questions and statements used in the Baltimore study. For clarity only the significant correlations are noted. The complete matrix is given in Appendix C.

In this particular matrix there are 220 possible correlations. A correlation is significant when the possibility of its occurring by chance is less than 5 percent ($p < .05$). Obviously, in a matrix of this size, as many as 11 correlations may seem significant but in fact be spurious. There are 94 correlations, or 63 percent of the possible total that are significant at the .05 level. Seventy-three, or 33 percent of all possible correlations, are significant at the .01 level.

Thus, at first sight, there does indeed seem to be a somewhat coherent set of negative attitudes toward the mentally ill. However, a closer inspection of the results shows this finding to be false.

In chapter 5 it was shown that the majority of respondents answered these questions in an "enlightened" manner. Therefore the correlations must represent consistency among the "enlightened" at least as frequently as they do among the rejective answers. Accordingly, the coherence of the consistency of response is at least as likely to be indicative of a coherent set of attitudes among those not rejecting the mentally ill as the reverse. Were this not so some correlations at least would be negative, and there were no negative correlations.

Another way in which the pattern of correlations fails to support the theory of rejection is the substantial number of significant correlations that exist between the home-care questions and the attitude statements. Many more people favored home care than did not. There is no way in which the willingness to retain a psychiatric patient at home can be explained as rejection. At best it must appear as a sporadic and idiosyncratic response. Yet this is the response that is consistent with "enlightened" replies given to the attitude statements.

Finally, answers to the identification questions seem to be largely unrelated to responses to any other question or statement. This is confirmed by the results of a canonical correlation between the identification questions and other questions and statements (table 23). A canonical correlation expresses the maximum possible relationship between two sets of variables

TABLE 22. Matrix of Significant Correlations Among Twenty-One Selected

Question/Statement	2	3	4	7-1	7-2	7-3	7-4	7-5	12-1
Identification questions									
2. Simple schizophrenic	1.00	0.24	0.18	*	*	*	*	0.10	*
3. Alcoholic		1.00	0.15	*	*	0.12	*	*	*
4. Paranoid			1.00	*	*	*	*	*	*
Attitude statements									
7-1. Not marry mentally ill				1.00	0.29	0.35	0.19	0.16	0.12
7-2. Could love mentally ill					1.00	0.39	0.25	0.10	0.18
7-3. Room with mentally ill						1.00	0.33	0.28	0.15
7-4. Work with mentally ill							1.00	0.21	0.16
7-5. Might work in mental hospital								1.00	*
12-1. Hospitalize all mentally ill									1.00
12-2. Most mentally ill are dangerous									
12-3. Guard mentally ill in institution									
12-4. Lock up mentally ill patients									
12-5. Many kinds of mentally ill									
12-6. All mentally ill act alike									
12-7. Some mental patients need home care									
12-8. Sometimes home care for mental patients									
12-9. If family member mentally ill, needs home care									
12-10. Mental patients are not criminal									
Home-care questions									
13. Depressed									
14. Involutional depression									
15. Senile									

*Indicates $r < .08$, $p > .05$.

NOTE: See Appendix A for text of questions.

Responses of 1,738 Respondents (Baltimore, 1960)

12-2	12-3	12-4	12-5	12-6	12-7	12-8	12-9	12-10	13	14	15	
*	*	*	*	*	*	*	*	*	*	*	*	2.
*	*	*	*	*	*	*	*	*	*	*	*	3.
*	*	*	0.08	*	*	*	*	*	*	*	*	4.
0.21	0.23	0.22	*	*	0.09	*	*	0.10	*	*	*	7-1.
0.19	0.17	0.18	*	*	*	*	*	0.11	0.11	*	*	7-2.
0.21	0.26	0.21	0.09	*	*	*	*	0.10	*	*	*	7-3.
0.23	0.20	0.23	*	0.16	*	0.11	0.11	*	*	*	*	7-4.
*	*	*	*	*	*	*	*	*	*	*	*	7-5.
0.41	0.39	0.34	*	0.22	0.24	0.28	0.19	0.12	0.18	0.18	0.17	12-1.
1.00	0.36	0.36	*	0.22	0.11	0.15	0.12	0.08	0.13	*	0.10	12-2.
	1.00	0.45	*	0.14	*	0.15	0.11	*	0.11	*	0.10	12-3.
		1.00	*	0.24	0.09	0.11	0.09	*	0.21	0.10	0.13	12-4.
			1.00	0.18	0.08	0.08	0.10	*	*	*	*	12-5.
				1.00	0.10	*	*	*	*	*	*	12-6.
					1.00	0.41	0.37	0.13	0.17	0.10	*	12-7.
						1.00	0.41	0.09	0.19	0.08	*	12-8
							1.00	0.08	0.16	0.08	*	12-9.
								1.00	*	*	*	12-10.
									1.00	0.32	0.15	13.
										1.00	0.23	14.
											1.00	15.

(Harman 1960; Hotelling 1936). The canonical R shown in table 23 fails to attain any reasonable level of significance. This can only support the conclusion that a population's ability to identify mental illness and its attitudes toward the mentally ill are two independent dimensions. Consequently, theories

TABLE 23. Canonical Correlation Between Identification Questions and Fifteen Attitudinal Statements

Canonical R (No Roots Removed)	Wilk's Lambda for Total Set	Associated Chi Square	n	p
0.19	0.93	51.25	45	less than 0.25

like the Cummings' where the concept of denial postulates such a relationship are unsupported.

The Factor Analysis

In order to reduce the massive correlation matrix, the matrix was subjected to a factor analysis. The particular type of factor analysis used was of the principal-factor type (Harman 1960, pp. 154–91). This type of factor analysis, derived with great mathematical rigor, accounts for the variance of a correlation matrix by a minimum set of components so that the correlation within the components is at a maximum, and the correlation between the components at a minimum. Thus a number of sets of items may be discussed rather than the response to each item. These sets—or more precisely the meaning they have in common—may be considered the dimensions or the underlying structure of the entire matrix. We found that seven factors explained 99 percent of the total variance of the matrix. These factors are unusually clear for an analysis of this sort, with a rather high degree of interrelatedness among the key statements making up each factor.

The Social-Distance Factor

The first factor consists of five statements requiring responses agreeing or disagreeing with specific social-distance attitudes:

We should strongly discourage our children from marrying anyone who has been mentally ill. 46% disagree

I can imagine myself falling in love with a person who had been mentally ill. 51% agree

I would be willing to room with someone who had been a patient in a mental hospital. 50% agree

I *wouldn't* hesitate to work with someone who had been mentally ill. 81% agree

If I could do the job and the pay were right, I wouldn't mind working in a mental hospital. 68% agree

The existence of an independent factor of social distance supports the claim that social proximity is a crucial element in attitudes toward the mentally ill, but the generally favorable responses indicate that a tolerance of minimal social distance is a characteristic of generally "enlightened" attitudes. The converse interpretation would, of course, be equally valid. The unambiguous point shown by the factor analysis is that social distance is simply one factor in a complex of attitudes.

The Family-Centeredness Factor

The second factor includes the three general statements about taking care of a mentally ill person at home. They are:

People who have some kinds of mental illness can be taken care of at home. 84% agree

Sometimes it is better for a person with a mental illness to live with his or her family instead of being in a mental hospital. 74% agree

If someone living in the same family with me became mentally ill, I would certainly try to take care of them at home if the doctor thought it wouldn't do any harm. 83% agree

The appearance of these three statements as a separate factor independent of the social-distance statements on the one hand and the responses to the home-care vignettes on the other must mean that there is a dimension of public attitudes independent of those determining responses to other statements.

Since there is another factor which seems to include the medical and social aspects of home care, it appears that the common element of maintaining family solidarity or family centeredness is involved here. The tendency of the family structure to resist disruption by external forces has been noted before in somatic illnesses (Hospital Council of Greater New York 1956) as well as in mental illness (Freeman and Simmons 1963; Grad and Sainsbury 1963). The Cummings also discussed the unwillingness of a family to admit a member's need for mental hospitalization (1957). They explained this in terms of the stigma of mental illness, but the independence of this family-centeredness factor from the social-distance factor makes it more likely that much of that resistance was to the disruption of the family per se.

The Home-Care Factor

The high loadings in this factor are the responses to the three vignettes discussed in chapter 5 and reproduced in Appendix A as questions 13, 14, and 15. These vignettes describe hypothetical mentally ill persons and ask the respondents whether the patient's family should hospitalize him or take care of him at home with the physician leaving the decision to them. In the Baltimore study about as many choices were made in favor of home care as were made for hospitalization.

The appearance of the three home-care vignettes in a separate factor indicates that the acceptance of home care is not a question of social distance, family solidarity, or even simple antihospital feelings. Although these statements are strongly correlated with the other attitude statements, it seems likely that they represent a general attitude about home care as such. Such items as whether the mentally ill are really sick are distinct though not unrelated matters.

To test the extent of the relationship between the answers to the home-care vignettes and the rest of the material in the questionnaire a canonical correlation was computed. The results are shown in table 24. The results demonstrate that

TABLE 24. Canonical Correlation Between Three Home-Care Questions and Eighteen Other Items

Number of Roots Removed	Corresponding Canonical R	Lambda	Chi Square	n	p
0	0.33	0.85	120.47	54	less than 0.001
1	0.16	0.95	36.84	34	less than 0.25

there is at least one way in which the answers to the home-care questions were very significantly related to the results obtained by the same analysis with the identification questions (table 23). Accordingly, whatever else they may represent, the answers to the home-care questions are clearly part of an interrelated set of attitudes about the mentally ill.

The Identification of Mental Illness

The identification of mental illness is the key to the questions in the fourth factor, and is represented in the answers, to the three Star vignettes shown in Appendix A as questions 2, 3, and 4, and discussed in chapter 3. Given the discorrelation of the identification questions, it is not surprising that they form a separate factor. What is surprising is that they form a different factor from the statements testing the stereotypy of the public's attitudes toward the mentally ill which appear in another factor. This means that the ability to recognize mental illness in specific cases is not one end of a continuum with stereotyping at the other. Some people may not stereotype the mentally ill, even if those people are unable to recognize the symptoms of illness. (The reverse, of course, is equally possible.)

The Nature of Hospitalization

The nature of hospitalization is the fifth factor. It consists of the following statements:

Everyone who has a mental illness should be placed in a mental hospital. 57% disagree

Every mental hospital should be surrounded by a high fence and guards. 62% disagree

The best way to handle people in mental hospitals is to keep them behind locked doors. 77% disagree

Almost all people who have a mental illness are dangerous. 75% disagree

The three statements that explicitly make mental hospitals the subject are all antirestraint in tone.

Four statements have high loadings in the hospitalization factor. As might be expected, these include the three which explicitly mention mental hospitals. The fourth statement is "almost all" persons who have a mental illness are dangerous. The combination of these statements in one factor might indicate that if one does not believe all mentally ill people are dangerous, one also does not believe mental hospitals should resemble prisons, or perhaps vice versa. One seeming anomaly is the "danger" statement which is included in the hospitalization factor, while the statement about a mentally ill person's criminality is not. Although a majority of the respondents found the mentally ill to be neither dangerous nor criminal, they were apparently significantly different majorities. Evidently the terms "criminal" and "dangerous" are part of two different dimensions in the public mind as far as the mentally ill are concerned.

The finding that attitudes about hospitals are an independent factor in attitudes toward the mentally ill is a strong confirmation of the contentions of people such as Hunt, who has long argued such a relationship (1958). However, the actual public acceptance of the mentally ill directly contradicts Hunt's further contention that "the custodial culture within the hospital is largely created by public pressure for security" (p. 9). The actual sequence might well be the reverse—namely, it is the custodial practice of the hospital that creates the public pressure for security.

Diversity of Mental Illness

The factor diversity of mental illness has its highest loadings in the two statements intended to test stereotypy. These are:

There are many different kinds of mental illness. 92% agree

All people with the same mental illness act in the same way. 83% disagree

Originally it was intended to term this factor stereotypy, but with such overwhelming popular perception of the heterogeneous nature of mental illness, such nomenclature would simply imply a nonexistent construct. The public is aware that there are many different categories of mental illness and that not even all of those with the same diagnosis behave in the same manner. We have already commented on the logical significance of the noncorrelation of these responses with the responses given to the identification questions.

Obviously from the occurrence of the two items in the same factor, the responses to the two statements are highly linked and awareness plays a role in the attitude toward the mentally ill. However, the unipolar nature of the factor and the large majorities endorsing the statement make it logically impossible to infer that there also exists a factor of "stereotypy." The absence of the awareness that there are many different kinds of mental illness and that not all persons with the same mental illness act in the same way would not necessarily mean that the public stereotyped the mentally ill. The existence of the factor on the other hand clearly indicates the absence of stereotyping. Consequently, evidence to support the great importance of stereotyping stated in such arguments as the "theory of rejection" is simply not to be found.

Criminality

The final factor has a significant loading in only the one statement about the criminality of former state mental hospital patients as opposed to other people. The statement is:

People who have been in a state mental hospital are no more likely to commit crimes than people who have never been in a state mental hospital. 59% agree

Probably the most important aspect of this factor, other than its existence, is that it explains the smallest amount of the variance of any factor. Therefore, it may be reasonably inferred that public concern about the possible criminal behavior of former mental hospital patients does not play a crucial role in attitudes toward the mentally ill. This again contradicts Hunt as quoted above.

Conclusions

The correlation-matrix and canonical-correlation analyses of the data from the Baltimore study show a high degree of intercorrelation between responses to various attitudinal statements (table 22). This is suggestive of a coherent and consistent attitude toward the mentally ill. The questions testing the ability of a respondent to recognize mental illness do not seem to be correlated with the attitudinal statements (tables 22 and 23). A principal-component analysis results in the reduction of the intercorrelations to seven uncorrelated principal factors (table 24). These factors are: nature of hospitalization, family centeredness, social distance, home versus hospital care, recognition of mental illness, diversity of mental illness, and criminality of the mentally ill. The structure that this analysis finds for attitudes toward the mentally ill is as much at variance with the structure posited by the "theory of rejection" as the "raw" responses to the attitude statements were opposed to the conclusion that the mentally ill are stigmatized and strongly rejected. According to the "theory of rejection," the public's attitudes are characterized by a pattern of denial, isolation, and rejection, stemming from fear of the mentally ill, stereotyped beliefs about them, and approval of the mental hospital as a prisonlike restraining institution. Although a number of different structures might be inferred from the principal-factor analysis, this is not one of them.

The essential elements of stereotypy diversity and denial-recognition are present, but of relatively little importance, while the factor of isolation of the mentally ill, though possible through inference from the structure of the statements, is not present in the responses. Indeed, the positive factors of family centeredness and home care versus hospitalization are contradictory to isolation.

There is no certitude that any factor analysis completely isolates all of the possible factors of the public's attitudes toward the mentally ill. It can only describe the factors included in the original matrix. The factor can be relevant and significant only to the extent that the elements of that matrix—the statements themselves—are relevant and significant. The Baltimore study was neither designed nor intended to be a thorough study of popular attitudes toward the mentally ill. It was limited to the population's readiness to accept home care of psychiatric patients. Positive inferences from this analysis must therefore be somewhat limited.

The same is not true of negative inferences. While it cannot be assumed that these factors are all the factors that play a part in the structure of public attitudes toward the mentally ill, nor that the addition of more refined statements might not alter the structure of various factors, further simplification by the addition of new elements is extremely unlikely. Thus the most important and most soundly based conclusion to be drawn from the factor analysis is that public attitudes toward the mentally ill are not unitary, or reducible to a simplistic triad. They are complex in structure and include a considerable range of factors of which rejection-acceptance is only one. Investigations and conclusions which presume simplicity in this area may well be defective in their design and thus unable to produce valid results.

Summary of the Data

It has been shown in chapter 3 that the public does not fail to recognize psychiatric symptoms as indicative of mental illness; in chapter 4, that it does not deny contact with people it knows to be mentally ill and that in fact such contact is common throughout the population studied; in chapter 5, that the public gives humane, enlightened, and nonpunitive responses to statements about the mentally ill; and in chapter 6, that it does not seek excessive social distance between itself and the former mental patient. It has been demonstrated that these attitudes are widespread, persistent through time, and most widely held by the younger portions of the population. Finally, in this chapter we have seen that these positive attitudes are complex, internally consistent, and not related to the ability to recognize mental illness. Accordingly, it seems that the theory of rejection as defined in chapter 2 has very little current substantive empirical foundation.

The implications of the failure of the "theory of rejection" for sociological theory are clear. There can be no social system without rejection of social deviance. Accordingly, the absence of substantial social rejection of the mentally ill means that the unqualified characterization of mental illness as simple social deviance is neither adequate nor scientifically accurate and that investigators of social response to social deviance must rely on other indices of deviant behavior.

CHAPTER 8

The Nature of Acceptance

The notion of rejection has so dominated professional thinking about public attitudes toward the mentally ill that it has formed the frame of reference within which almost all relevant social research has taken place. Although it might seem that the large volume of data inconsistent with the idea of rejection would make the construction of an empirically grounded alternative relatively simple, this has not been the case. The pervasive influence of the fundamental belief in the public rejection of the mentally ill is clearly reflected in every study reported in the literature. Neither the Baltimore study nor the first UAW survey was immune to this pervasive influence. Both studies attempted to measure social distance by the use of dichotomous material with the implicit assumption that the category, mentally ill, was perceived in an undifferentiated fashion by a relatively unsophisticated public. The results were interpreted without any baseline, arbitrarily assuming that any deviation from 100 percent acceptance represented some degree of rejection. One wonders whether anyone would postulate 100 percent acceptance of the physically ill and interpret any deviation as evidence of stigma, stereotypy, and rejection. This chapter concentrates on details of the data and observations whose significance may have been hidden because of the a priori assumption of rejection.

The Pattern of Acceptance

In the resurvey of the UAW sample, instead of proceeding with the assumption of rejection, it was decided to measure social acceptance of former mental patients. Acceptance was measured by comparing the acceptance accorded an individual without a history of mental hospitalization with a comparable individual with such a history.

An idealized "normal" individual was described as a referent. The following description was taken from the questionnaire used by Phillips (1963):

Here is a description of a man. Imagine that he is a respectable person living in your neighborhood. He is happy and cheerful, has a good enough job and is fairly well satisfied with it. He is always busy and has quite a few friends who think he is easy to get along with most of the time. Within the next few months he plans to marry a nice young woman he is engaged to.

Seventy-four randomly selected respondents were asked: "How would you feel about having someone like this for a neighbor? Would you say you're *definitely* willing, *probably* willing, *probably* unwilling, or *definitely* unwilling to have him as a neighbor?"

They were then asked the same questions about "admitting a person like this to a favorite club or organization," "working on the same job" with him, "renting a room in your home" to him, and "having one of your children marry" him.

Two hundred three randomly selected respondents were read the same description with the additional qualification that the referent had once been in a mental hospital. They were then asked the same social-distance questions. The description was as follows:

Here is a description of a man. He is generally healthy although he was once in a hospital for mental illness. He has a good enough job and is fairly well satisfied with it. He is always busy and has quite a few friends who think he is easy to get along with most of the time. Within the next few months he plans to marry a nice young woman he is engaged to.

One hundred eighty-seven randomly selected respondents were asked the same questions about a female former mental patient. The female referent was described in exactly the same words except that feminine pronouns were substituted throughout.

One hundred eighty-nine randomly selected respondents were asked the same questions, but the referent, instead of being one of the above cameos, was simply "someone who had been in a mental hospital."

The Pattern of Social Distance

Tables 25 through 28 detail the responses to the social-distance questions for each description. If table 25 is interpreted only dichotomously between those willing and unwilling, it is clear that there is some slight resistance to even the "normal" man. When these data are analyzed in terms of both definitely willing and probably willing, an entirely new dimension is revealed. The seemingly minor difference between marital and neighborly relationships now shows a 21 percent reduction in the definitely willing category. This phenomenon of strongly decreasing unconditional acceptance as the relationship becomes more intimate not only provides some insight into the nature of increased social distance, but also indicates the inadequacy of a dichotomous statement to accurately describe such changes. This is especially likely to occur in a survey-interview situation where interviewers conventionally are instructed to "pin the respondents down," "force choices from quibbles," and avoid "don't knows."

As can be seen in tables 26, 27, and 28, the major shifts that occur when the questions move from the less-intimate relationship of "working with" to the closer relationships of "renting a room to" and "having one of your children marry" are the shifts between definitely willing and probably willing, in other words, from unconditional to conditional acceptance. This is the same type of shift that occurred with the "normal" subject. Apparently when someone who has been mentally

TABLE 25. Percentage of UAW Respondents Willing to Accept Social Relationship with "Normal" Individual (Wave II)

Relationship	Total Willing	Definitely Willing	Probably Willing	Total Unwilling
Neighbor	100%	78%	22%	—
Club member	100	73	27	—
Work with	99	74	25	1%
Rent room to	91	55	36	9
Child marry	95	57	38	5

NOTE: N = 74.

TABLE 26. Percentage of UAW Respondents Willing to Accept Social Relationship with Male Former Patient (Wave II)

Relationship	Total Willing	Definitely Willing	Probably Willing	Probably Unwilling	Definitely Unwilling	Total Unwilling
Neighbor	98%	58%	40%	—	1%	1%
Club member	97	62	35	1%	1	2
Work with	97	62	35	1	1	2
Rent room to[a]	82	31	51	12	5	17
Child marry[a]	76	18	58	16	6	22

NOTE: N = 203. Percentages add to less than 100 because of rounding.
a. "Don't know" and "no answer" eliminated from tabulation.

ill is used as the referent, the shift is more pronounced than is the case with the "normal" referent.

This type of distribution of response might well be the pattern of acceptance in a multigroup and pluralistic society. It consists of a considerable amount of unconditional acceptance in the socially more distant relationships, irrespective of personal characteristics, and an increase of conditional acceptance, a "wait-and-see" response, in the socially closer relationships, again irrespective of the superficial personal

TABLE 27. Percentage of UAW Respondents Willing to Accept Social Relationship with Female Former Mental Patient (Wave II)

Relationship	Total Willing	Definitely Willing	Probably Willing	Probably Unwilling	Definitely Unwilling	Total Unwilling
Neighbor	97%	71%	26%	—	3%	3%
Club member	96	71	25	1%	3	4
Work with	97	72	25	—	3	3
Rent room to[a]	83	44	39	6	10	16
Child marry[a]	77	33	44	13	9	22

NOTE: N = 187. In some cases, percentages add to less than 100 because of rounding.

a. "Don't know" and "no answer" eliminated from tabulation.

TABLE 28. Percentage of UAW Respondents Willing to Accept Social Relationship with "Someone" Who Had Been a Former Mental Patient (Wave II)

Relationship	Total Willing	Definitely Willing	Probably Willing	Probably Unwilling	Definitely Unwilling	Total Unwilling
Neighbor	98%	54%	44%	—	1%	1%
Club member	98	56	42	1%	1	2
Work with	96	61	35	2	2	4
Rent room to[a]	79	24	55	12	8	20
Child marry[a]	63	12	51	23	12	35

NOTE: N = 189. In some cases, percentages add to less than 100 because of rounding.

a. "Don't know" and "no answer" eliminated from tabulation.

characteristics. If so, the acceptance of the former mental patient is qualitatively no different from that accorded the normal individual. There is, however, a quantitative difference in that the former mental patient encounters conditional acceptance with significantly greater frequency and unconditional acceptance with significantly less.

Acceptance Based on Referent Characteristics

In chapter 2 the importance of stereotyping to the theories of prejudice and stigma was shown. In chapters 3, 5, and 7, evidence was offered that the public does not stereotype the mentally ill but is well aware of the diversity of their traits. Therefore, a question wording that assumes an undifferentiated stereotype on the part of the public may well distort the true nature of the response. Descriptions such as "someone who has been mentally ill" or "someone who has been in a mental hospital" are of this type. Yet "someone" or "a person" is the most frequent referent used in surveys of social response to the mentally ill.

The same criticism might be made of the term *mental illness* or *mentally ill.* In chapters 4 and 5, evidence was offered to show that the public is aware that "there are many different kinds of mental illness."

The methodological assumption underlying such question wordings is that the respondents' unique biases and experiences will "wash out," permitting an overall assessment of response that is essentially unbiased. There is no evidence supporting such an assumption and the burden of proof is on those who maintain that these are indeed neutral categories. It is not sufficient to state that there are no obvious biases in the wording of a question any more than it is sufficient to assert the unbiased nature of a sample simply because of the absence of overt bias. Positive procedures to insure lack of bias are necessary in both cases.

In the instance of the blanket term, mental illness, the possibility of bias can be substantiated by both empirical and expert evidence. In the New York City study, after a series of social-distance questions about "a person . . . that had been . . . a patient in a mental hospital," respondents were asked: "If you found out *what kind* of mental illness the person had, how much difference would that make in your decision, one way or the other?" Only 19 percent of the respondents said that it would make no difference to them. Thirty-six percent said that it would make "much" difference to them, and 40 percent said that it would make "some" difference to them (Elinson, Padilla, Perkins 1967, p. 125).

Paul Lemkau writes:

> I have for many years been arguing that there is no such thing as mental illness, only mental illnesses which differ from each other to extreme degrees. In this sense "mental illness" is a myth, a composite of many reactions and reaction types each with more or less specific characteristics. The issue that needs to be further investigated . . . is what does the public think of this or that mental illness, not all mental illnesses. . . . Mental illness is a myth, but the mental illnesses is a logical collective name that has some limited usage. (P. Lemkau, personal communication)

In the instance of the undescribed referent "someone" in social-distance questions, the issue is more subtle. It might be maintained, for example, that the stigma of having suffered from one of the mental illnesses is so all encompassing that the presence or absence of any other characteristic is secondary and would at best modify the general response only slightly. This was the case, for instance, with the American blacks in 1942. At that time 72 percent of a sample objected to having "a Negro in their neighborhood." When asked essentially the same question in the following form: "If a Negro with just as much education and income as you have moved into your block would it make any difference to you?" The negative response was only slightly modified to 62 percent.

It might also be argued that the term "someone" is truly neutral and that adding any desirable or undesirable characteristics simply distorts the essential neutrality of the referent. Against this point it could be argued that simply saying "someone who has been mentally ill" without indicating the presence of any other conventional characteristics implies that the referent's past mental illness (an already questionable category) is the most important thing about him. Thus, in effect, a stereotypical response is forced, where no stereotype actually exists. If indeed the true measure of the extent of rejection of the mentally ill is the extent to which they fall short of achieving the acceptance accorded a "normal" person, then one must present some baseline against which to measure. The only equally "neutral" baseline for the description "someone who has been mentally ill" is "someone who has not been mentally ill." Social-distance questions with such a referent are an absurdity. In order to test the neutrality of the undescribed referent, "someone," it is necessary to approach the problem from the opposite direction. Three steps are necessary for this: 1) to describe a hypothetical individual and obtain social-distance responses to such a referent; 2) to add to as nearly the same description as possible the information that the individual had been a patient in a mental hospital and obtain social-distance responses to that referent from a different random group of respondents; and 3) using an undescribed "someone" who "had been a patient in a mental hospital," to obtain social-distance responses from a third randomly selected group.

The difference between responses to the referent who was not hospitalized and the same referent described as having been hospitalized would be the measure of the rejection due to mental hospitalization. Differences between the undescribed "someone" who was hospitalized and the described referent who was hospitalized would be the measure of the effect of the characterization. At the same time, the argument that the stigma of mental hospitalization is so all-encompassing that it overrides all other characteristics of the hospitalized individual would also be tested. Such a procedure was essentially followed in this study. The responses to the social-distance questions for each version of the referent and for each point of social distance are shown in tables 29 through 33.

In the three more distant social relationships of neighbor, club member, and workmate, there is no significant difference in overall willingness between responses to the "normal" and any of the former mental patients. Differences do become

TABLE 29. Percentage of UAW Members Willing to Have Referent As Neighbor (Wave II)

Willingness	Normal (N = 74)	Female Patient (N = 187)	Male Patient (N = 203)	"Someone" Patient (N = 189)
Definitely willing	78%	71%	58%	54%
Probably willing	22	26	40	44
Probably unwilling	—	—	—	—
Definitely unwilling	—	3	1	1
Don't know	—	—	1	1
	Definitely willing vs. probably willing compared with normal			
X^2 =		0.8	8.5	12.09
P =		<.75	<.005	<.001

TABLE 30. Percentage of UAW Members Willing to Have Referent in Favorite Club or Organization (Wave II)

Willingness	Normal (N = 74)	Female Patient (N = 187)	Male Patient (N = 203)	"Someone" Patient (N = 189)
Definitely willing	73%	71%	62%	56%
Probably willing	27	25	35	42
Probably unwilling	—	1	1	1
Definitely unwilling	—	3	1	1
Don't know	—	—	1	—
	Definitely willing vs. probably willing compared with normal			
X^2 =		0.000	1.638	4.856
P =		<.99	<.20	<.05

TABLE 31. Percentage of UAW Members Willing to Work with Referent (Wave II)

Willingness	Normal (N = 74)	Female Patient (N = 187)	Male Patient (N = 203)	"Someone" Patient (N = 189)
Definitely willing	73%	72%	62%	61%
Probably willing	26	25	35	35
Probably unwilling	—	—	1	2
Definitely unwilling	—	3	1	2
Don't know	1	—	1	—
	Definitely willing vs. probably willing compared with normal			
X^2 =		0.016	2.547	2.6724
P =		<.90	<.20	<.20

TABLE 32. Percentage of UAW Members Willing to Rent Room to Referent (Wave II)

Willingness	Normal (N = 74)	Female Patient (N = 187)	Male Patient (N = 203)	"Someone" Patient (N = 189)
Definitely willing	55%	44%	31%	24%
Probably willing	36	39	51	55
Probably unwilling	3	6	12	12
Definitely unwilling	9	10	5	8
Don't know	—	1	1	1
	Definitely willing vs. probably willing compared with normal			
X^2 =		1.04	9.9778	17.7
P =		<.5	<.005	<.001
	All willing vs. all unwilling compared with normal			
P =		<.25	<.30	<.025

TABLE 33. Percentage of UAW Members Willing to Have Child Marry Referent (Wave II)

Willingness	Normal (N = 74)	Female Patient (N = 187)	Male Patient (N = 203)	"Someone" Patient (N = 189)
Definitely willing	57%	33%	18%	12%
Probably willing	38	44	58	51
Probably unwilling	1	13	16	23
Definitely unwilling	1	9	6	12
Don't know	3	1	2	1
	Difference between normal and former patients answering willing vs. probably willing			
X^2 =		5.41378	27.627	32.31232
P =		<.025	<.001	<.001
	Difference between normal and former patients answering willing vs. unwilling compared with normal			
P =		<.05	<.001	<.001

apparent when "definitely willing" responses are compared to "probably willing" responses for these same relationships. There are no significant differences between responses to the "normal" referent and the female mental patient. There are differences, however, for the male patient and the referent described as "someone." Both are significantly less desirable as neighbors. The undescribed referent—"someone"—is also significantly less desirable as a club member.

The difference becomes more pronounced in the closer social relationships of "rent room to" and "having one of your children marry." There is no significant difference between general willingness to rent a room to either the female or male former mental patient, and willingness to rent to the "normal" person. There is a significantly greater reluctance to rent a room to the uncharacterized former mental patient, "someone."

When "definitely willing" responses are compared to "probably willing" responses for the above relationship for the three subjects, further differences become evident. Although there is still no significant difference between the female former mental patient and the "normal" person, there is a significant difference between the responses accorded the male former patient and the "normal" person. Acceptance is more conditional for the male patient.

The relationship involved in "having one of your children marry" requires acceptance of maximal social intimacy in our scale. A majority of respondents were willing to accept such a relationship with each of three former mental patients. However, the acceptance was significantly greater for the "normal" referent.

The differences are slightly more marked when those responding "definitely willing" versus "probably willing" are compared. There are significantly fewer "definitely willing" responses for all three former mental patients.

The tabulations (tables 29 through 33) demonstrate that mental hospitalization is not such an overriding characteristic as to nullify all other characteristics of an individual insofar as response to social-distance questions is concerned. They also show that the difference in response to the social-distance questions that can logically be attributed to the experience of mental hospitalization (i.e., the difference between the male former mental patient and the individual described in identical terms who had *not* been hospitalized) varies significantly from that obtained when the referent "someone" is used. The referent "someone" consistently secures less accepting responses than either of the other described referents. Therefore, the ability of the referent "someone" to secure unbiased response, that is, its neutrality, is questionable. Finally, the attribution of specific characteristics to the referent, even simple and apparently neutral characteristics such as sex, significantly alters the responses to the social-distance questions.

The considerable effect of including in the description of a referent such variables as sex, social class, income, education, physical characteristics, or a history of physical illness can easily be inferred from the tabulations shown in Appendix B. For example, in this sample, among those under thirty years of age who responded to the referent of the female mental patient, a higher proportion were definitely willing to have her as a daughter-in-law than were willing to have the similarly described "normal" referent as a son-in-law. The occurrence of such differences means that the social characteristics of the population and the social characteristics of the ex-mental patient can be more important than the fact of mental hospitalization itself.

Substantiating such a hypothesis would have important clinical and sociological implications. Clinically it would confirm in another way some of the findings of Freeman and Simmons (1963) concerning the return of the mental patient to the community. It would provide the therapist with an additional dimension of interpretation of patient rejection and acceptance.

Sociologically the substantiation of such a hypothesis implies that social response to any categorized behavior cannot be studied adequately in a vacuum. As indicated by evidence from other areas of sociological inquiry, such as criminology, drug use, delinquency, and indeed mental illness itself, the social characteristics of the actor and the population powerfully modify social response to both behavior and role (Hollingshead and Redlich 1958).

Conclusions

Evidence has been presented to:

1. Suggest that the pattern of acceptance of both a "normal" referent and a former mental patient in a social relationship

consists of an increase in conditional acceptance as the relationship approaches family membership

2. Demonstrate that the characteristics attributed to a hypothetical ex-mental patient significantly modify response to social-distance questions concerning the patient

3. Suggest that the proper measure of acceptance of former mental patients is the extent to which the response to an ex-patient with certain characteristics differs from the response to a referent with no hospital history but having identical characteristics

4. Suggest that for defined groups in the population the attribution of specific characteristics to a referent that was formerly mentally ill will result in social-distance answers not significantly different from those given a referent with no history of mental illness described in a similar manner

The above conclusions are all related to the acceptance-rejection continuum of the mentally ill. As has been suggested earlier, the implications are broader. If subsequent research should substantiate the hypothesis for the mentally ill, then it would be a reasonable inference that the same pattern might be found for other general categories and roles. The implications of such findings are that social acceptance or rejection of general behaviors and roles is significantly contingent on the sociological characteristics of the actors, on the one hand, and significantly independent of their normative categorization on the other.

PART III

Acceptance or Rejection

CHAPTER 9

Behavioral Acceptance of Mental Illness

The point of departure for this work was the general proposition that the mentally ill are stereotyped, stigmatized, and punitively rejected by society. Data have been offered that contradict this proposition.

The data reviewed in this book indicate that people are almost unanimous in believing that the mentally ill are truly sick and thus require medical treatment "just as any other sick person" does. The public believes that there are many different kinds of mental illness and that persons suffering from the same kind of mental illness do not necessarily behave in the same manner. Most people recognize descriptions of specific behavior patterns as symptomatic of illness, and close social contact with known mentally ill persons is common and freely admitted.

People believe that some of the mentally ill can be cared for at home and, as far as their own choice is concerned, would prefer to take care of a mentally ill family member at home if it were not medically detrimental to him. They do not believe that most mentally ill are dangerous nor do they believe that the mentally ill are especially prone to criminal behavior. Quite consistently they do not believe that mental patients should be "locked up" or that mental hospitals should be fenced off and guarded.

The public believes to the point of consensus that the mentally ill can be cured with proper treatment, and almost all are quite willing to accept people who have been severely mentally ill as neighbors, fellow club members, and workmates. A majority are willing to accept former mental patients as family members. Such nonacceptance as exists is not qualitatively different from that accorded someone without a history of hospitalization. Acceptance simply tends to be more provisional. The individual characteristics of the former mental patient significantly affect the degree of acceptance.

The overwhelming evidence that support is lacking for the "theory of rejection" in survey data may be countered by the argument that survey responses do not reflect social reality or actual social behavior. However, since data obtained by similar methodology provide the key empirical basis for the "theory of rejection," the argument so far has been restricted to this type of evidence. In this chapter, the "soft data' of recent historical behavior patterns toward the mentally ill will be briefly examined.

Changes in State Mental Hospitals

For the last twenty years there has been a gradual and yet dramatic change in the role of state mental hospitals. The shift has been from a custodial position to that of a treatment position; that is, the primary function of the state hospital is now considered to be a medical obligation to the patient rather than a *de facto* social obligation to protect society by the incarceration of the mentally ill. This evolution from a custodial, restrictive, and punitive jaillike role to a therapeutic role was greatly accelerated by the introduction of psychoactive drugs, particularly the phenothiazines, in the mid-1950s. The growing recognition of the rehabilitative potential of even the most desperately sick patient changed the picture of the patient from a hopeless creature doomed to become a burden on society to that of a person entitled to the sick role. The sick role allows socially approved temporary abdication of responsibilities, with the expectation of eventual return to the status, position, and social responsibility maintained by the patient before the illness.

The expectation that any patient admitted to a public psychiatric hospital would while away the remainder of his days in the hospital or at least spend a good many years of his life there has changed to that of a temporary sojourn, with discharge within months becoming the rule rather than the exception. The majority of the patients in the 1960s have been discharged within six months of admission.

Would such profound changes have been possible in the face of widespread public opposition? With hundreds of thousands of patients being released from mental hospitals annually, society's feelings about mental illness and society's attitudes toward former mental hospital patients have had ample opportunity for concrete expression. Had the dark apocalyptic vision of society basic to the "theory of rejection" been actualized, had employers refused to hire ex-patients, had landlords refused to accept them as tenants, had people refused to work alongside them or to allow their children to marry them—in short, had they not been allowed to resume their role as members of the society from which they had been removed to be hospitalized—there should by now exist a sizable isolated, and discriminated against, outgroup of ex-mental hospital patients.

Another result of the change from the custodial to the treatment model of mental hospitals has been the institution of open wards. Until about twenty years ago, virtually all of the mental patients in the United States were kept in locked wards. This policy was often defended on the grounds that the public expected to be carefully protected from mental patients. Gradually, but progressively, locks have been removed from the doors of many wards in mental hospitals. Time and time again, the trepidation of the administrative staff of many hospitals with regard to public outcry has been shown to be unfounded.

An equally dramatic shift has been taking place in the nature of admission to state mental hospitals. This shift has been from one where all patients were committed involuntarily by judicial order to one of patients voluntarily seeking admission to hospitals. Throughout the country, for example, both the absolute number and proportion of voluntary admissions have shown such remarkable increases that at present the majority of patients being hospitalized are admitted on a voluntary basis. Such a shift is clearly inconsistent with the conception of the mental hospital as an instrument for the punitive sanction of deviant behavior.

It is generally agreed that these changes are insufficient, have been slow in coming, and are long overdue. It is also generally agreed that some state hospitals remain prisonlike anachronistic devices for hiding mental patients from society. However, what is relevant to this discussion is that wherever the above changes have taken place, they have taken place with minimal opposition by the public. In fact, in many instances, public groups such as mental health associations have had a significant role in exerting pressure to bring about these changes. Resistance has sometimes come from the administrative and professional staff of the institutions rather than from the society at large. It may be speculated that belief in the "theory of rejection" has played some role in the resistance. After all, the public psychiatric institutions are dependent almost totally on the public for financial support. The public is presumably paying "protection money." It has been willing to pay so that the mentally ill may be removed from society and incarcerated in institutions. What if the public would not go along with these changes? What if the public demanded that mental hospitals remain custodial, or at best demanded such strict safeguards before a patient could be discharged that it would be impossible for all practical purposes to discharge many patients? What an awkward, painful choice would then confront the mental health professional: betrayal of his patients and his professional ethics on the one hand, or the loss of his position and livelihood on the other. In theory at least, in a democratic society, it is the public who bestows the right and the privilege of the position to professionals, the public then has the power to withdraw this privilege.

What is the available evidence? No reform-minded state hospital superintendent has been burned in effigy; not a single state mental hospital has been taken away from the mental health professionals and handed over to wardens; nor has a single hospital been picketed by an irate populace. No candidate has been elected to state or federal legislature on a platform of returning a state mental hospital to its previous custodial position. Such attacks as have occurred from the far right do not support, but oppose, custodial care. Federal and state expenditures for treatment of the mentally ill have regularly increased year after year. Budget-conscious states have even sacrificed needed funds for state hospitals while seeking to sustain embryonic outpatient and community programs. Such behavior is hardly consistent with the rejection hypothesis.

The Increasing Role of the General Hospital

One of the most interesting trends in the inpatient treatment of the mentally ill is that by the late 1960s, more than half the annual admissions for mental illness have been to general hospitals. There is little question that the public views the general hospitals as institutions for the short-term care and cure of the acutely ill. There has been no reported public outcry against the use of scarce general hospital beds for the treatment of the mentally ill. In fact, there has been a rising demand that more general hospitals accept mental patients. The statistical evidence verifying that, at present, the majority of those hospitalized annually for mental illness are admitted to general hospitals permits several inferences: 1) that the society does not conceive of the mentally ill as deviants but rather as sick people; 2) that both the hospital and general public conceive of the mentally ill as curable in a relatively short time, 3) that the public prefers treatment for the mentally ill rather than isolation and punishment, and 4) neither the hospital society nor the larger society harbors stereotypes of the mentally ill as dangerous and violent. Such stereotypes would not permit, in the general-hospital setting, the close association of the mentally ill with physically helpless sick patients.

Community Mental Health Centers

Public support in the past twenty years of a whole complex of activities to provide alternatives to hospitalization with emphasis on early treatment, rehabilitation, and other measures to prevent chronicity culminated in 1963 in the adoption by Congress of the Community Mental Health Centers Act, authorizing the appropriation of federal funds to support the development of mental health programs located within the communities where the patients and their families lived. There are at present over four hundred community mental health centers, either in operation, under construction, or with the final planning approved. Future plans call for many more, though defense expenditures have barred sufficient funding. These centers represent an extensive financial commitment on the part of all levels of government, and a strong intent to provide treatment for the mentally ill within the community rather than in remote mental hospitals. This can hardly be considered as compatible with any of the tenets of the "theory of rejection."

Other Factors

Other developments that are incompatible with the "theory of rejection"—too numerous to detail—reflect the forces influencing the shape and direction of the mental health movement in the past twenty years. These include the institution of convalescent leave from state mental hospitals with the establishment of aftercare programs within communities, foster-care programs, expansion of outpatient services for the mentally ill, establishment of crisis clinics and the involvement of the mental health professionals in various public institutions such as schools, departments of social services, courts, and more. For each halfway house involving a zoning-board protest, dozens have been quiety received. New modalities of therapy, such as short-term psychotherapy, group therapies, and crisis intervention, have made it possible to provide psychiatric care for a much larger number of patients. Inclusion of mental illness in health-insurance programs has also been a development of the recent years. By 1965, four out of every five of the Blue Cross Association's sixty-two million members had some degree of coverage for "nervous and mental disorders." Inclusion of psychiatric treatment in the prepaid medical insurance plans has made it possible for a large number of lower-middle-class and working-class people to receive private psychiatric care.

Conclusion

It is hazardous to interpret historical trends without the perspective gained by the passage of time. Still it is difficult to imagine how one could claim that the behavioral data of the past decade support a rejection hypothesis. Disappointments in funding of community programs, occasional protest about opening a mental health facility in a neighborhood, discrimination in insurance policies, and other hindrances might be taken out of context to build a case. However, many social programs proceed at less than optimal speed; zoning protests are directed at virtually any neighborhood construction other than private dwellings; and outpatient-medical, tuberculosis-hospital, and retarded-child benefits are commonly excluded from insurance packages. The predominant trends in state hospital care patterns, general hospital psychiatric units, and community mental health centers seem incompatible with the rejection hypothesis.

CHAPTER 10

The Theory of Rejection: Appeal and Consequences

The persistence of belief in the "theory of rejection" among many mental health professionals raises a fundamental question, namely: What are the roots of such belief? Consider a psychiatrist in general practice. What factors help shape his opinion about the public's attitude toward his patients? The more prominent of the multitude of factors can be speculatively summarized into: his own personal experiences, his training, his contact with his patients, his contact with his colleagues, his contact with the community at large, and the influence of professional literature (discussed in chapters 1 and 2).

Personal Experiences

Many mental health professionals have a great deal of personal experience with social rejection and ostracism. Many of us come from minority groups and may have experienced peer-group rejection during critical, formative years. We may be all too prone to see the outside world as composed of ranks closed against the sensitive, the injured, and the emotionally disturbed. Others find the position of being the protector of downtrodden, rejected, and discriminated-against patients as an ennobling and satisfying position. Mental health professionals as a group may be more liberal and more identified with minority-group cultures than other professional groups (*Biographical Directory* 1968) and hence may experience a quixotic sense of mission in serving as protectors. Indeed, such attitudes may even have functional utility in creating a willingness to treat people whose behaviors are sometimes unpleasant. On the other hand, there is the difficulty that the position of the protector of the downtrodden demands there be someone who is downtrodden. It is quite conceivable that the mental health professional is locked into a social role that demands that the data concerning the shift in public attitudes be ignored.

Training

The impact of training is far-reaching. So long as those who teach medical students and psychiatric residents are convinced that there is widespread public stigma concerning mental illness, the error is compounded. Accepted myths fall as hard in psychiatry as in any other field. Standard textbooks such as Freedman and Kaplan continue to teach the "theory of rejection" uncritically. The correction for such attitudes should come from the reports of research findings in professional articles and presentations. However, many of the written signposts pointing to research in this field are so diffusely distributed in the professional literature that only the academician with a specialized interest can avail himself of the cumulative data. For most, a chance encounter is the rule rather than the exception. No wonder then the conclusions that the public "rejects the mentally ill, the psychiatric hospitals and the people who man them" drawn by the Joint Commission on Mental Illness and Health in its 1961 publication and based on findings from the 1950s continue to exert greater influence than the major studies reported in the 1960s showing contradictory evidence.

Contacts with Patients

The primary source of data for the practicing psychiatrist is his own contact with patients. Many patients suffer a sense of loneliness, alienation, and rejection as part of their illness. Patients from several different diagnostic categories may well tend to overreport societal rejection. For the paranoid, the assumption that the world is against him forms the core of his mental illness. Many schizoid patients need to view the community as hostile and rejecting to rationalize their self-imposed isolation and withdrawal. Projection of hostility, rejection, and negative attitudes to family members, neighbors, and the society at large is a major part of the symptomatology of many schizophrenic illnesses. Patients in the throes of depression are often guilt ridden and see themselves as so "soiled" as to be deserving of punishment and untouchable by society. Many neurotic patients are hypersensitive to the most minor slights and perceive them as major rejection. They are often too ready to explain personal failure in terms of the sins of parental surrogates (i.e., society at large). Feelings of alienation, separateness, and loneliness are highly prevalent among the mentally ill. Perhaps the early appellation for psychiatrists—"alienists"—was an apt one, for a preponderance of the patients surveyed in our studies expressed such feelings. Table 34 documents the loneliness experienced by a population

TABLE 34. Feelings of Loneliness Reported by Population Sample of United Auto Workers and by Clinic Patients of United Auto Workers (Wave I)

How often do you feel lonely?	UAW Population Sampled (N = 888)	UAW Clinic Patients (Active) (N = 30)
Most of the time	2%	27%
Pretty often	5	13
Just a little	25	37
Never	59	23
Don't know, no answer	8	—

NOTE: "Most of the time" and "Pretty often" combined; "just a little" and "Never" combined. $Chi^2 = 37.5456$.
$p < .01$.

of clinic patients compared with the nonclinic patients in the homogeneous group to which both the patients and nonpatients belonged (UAW population and their spouses). It is to be emphasized that these patients come from the population whose nonrejecting attitudes are documented in this volume.

The patient population's sense of isolation is demonstrated in table 35, and the patients' sense of separateness even when at social gatherings is shown in table 36. Similar studies done on a patient population with more chronic forms of mental illness, in the Henry Phipps Outpatient Psychiatric Service, provide even more striking confirmation of the loneliness and isolation which forms part of the feeling experience of many patients with psychiatric illnesses (Siassi, Crocetti, Spiro 1973).

Many patients feel a sense of self-hatred and disgust for their symptoms when mentally ill. This ego-dystonic aspect of neurotic symptomatology is a powerful spur toward recovery. However, the very quality of hating the symptoms that bring the patient to medical attention may distort the patient's view of how others feel about him. He often assumes that if he himself hates and rejects his symptoms so strongly, then others must also hate and reject those symptoms in him and, by extension, hate and reject him. Viewing the world through his patient's eyes, the psychiatrist is apt to see a distorted picture of the patient's community. This is especially so when the patient belongs to a different social milieu. Here, oftentimes, the psychiatrist's only view of the patient's society is through the window opened to him by the patient.

There are other incentives for the psychiatrist to maintain belief in the "theory of rejection." The theory allows the doctor and his patient to explain failure in treatment on the basis of unreasoning outside forces. The frustrations of unsuccessful therapy are difficult to accept. It is quite tempting to seek a scapegoat when progress is too slow. It is much less painful for both the therapist and the patient to feel indignation with the "biased" employer when the schizophrenic patient is turned down for a job, rather than to continue examining the psychotic

TABLE 35. Being Alone Reported by Population Sample of UAW and by Clinic Patients of UAW (Wave I)

How often are you alone more than you like to be?	UAW Population Sampled (N = 888)	UAW Clinic Patients (Active) (N = 30)
Most of the time	4%	17%
Pretty often	7	10
Just a little	20	37
Never	62	37
Don't know, no answer	8	—

NOTE: "Most of the time" and "Pretty often" combined; "Just a little" and "Never" combined: $Chi^2 = 5.8429$.
$p < .025$.

TABLE 36. Feeling of Being Apart from Others Reported by Population Sample of UAW and by Clinic Patients of UAW (Wave I)

How often do you have feelings of being apart from other people even when at a party or social gathering?	UAW Population Sampled (N = 888)	UAW Clinic Patients (Active) (N = 30)
Most of the time	1%	20%
Pretty often	2	23
Just a little	20	13
Never	69	43
Don't know, no answer	8	—

NOTE: "Most of the time" and "Pretty often" combined; "Just a little" and "Never" combined: $Chi^2 = 103.0479$.
$p < .01$.

behavior which may lead to such "rejection." The boring tedium and compulsive repetitiveness of those with obsessional character may cause lack of job advancement or social failures. But the therapist and his patient may find it easier to conclude that the cause of failure is a biased employer or a prejudiced social clique. The concept of hostile social response to the mentally ill may thus serve as a convenient scapegoat for both the therapist and the patient in some frustrating and difficult cases in therapy.

Another possible reason for the appeal of the "theory of rejection" is that many therapists find countertransference hatred difficult and unpleasant to face (Winnicott 1949). With such belief the therapist's countertransference hostility is easily projected onto the family and the larger society. The therapist's own repressed hostility and his tendency to reject the patient are projected onto the general public. Authoritative descriptions of the public as prejudiced and rejecting facilitate such projection. On a different level, the patients manifesting recalcitrant and hostile behavior make it difficult for the therapist to maintain his position of neutrality, understanding, and helpfulness. We have been particularly impressed with this phenomenon in supervising psychiatric residents who are treating rather unpleasant patients. Commonly, the family, school, and employers are cast in a malevolent light without any objective evidence.

Contact with Professional Colleagues

The medical profession is certainly not known for its acceptance of psychiatric disorders. In fact, it may be that attitudes among internists and surgeons are more negative than the reputed attitudes among the public at large. Through a training program laced with physical science and concern for physical illnesses, the practicing physician trained in the 1930's and 1940s is unlikely to have any broad sympathy for and understanding of psychiatric disorder. Physicians as a group may tend to be more conservative, judgmental, and unsympathetic concerning functional disorders than many other groups in society. Noticing hostile and derogatory attitudes concerning the psychiatrically ill in the hallowed halls of medical schools from esteemed and highly educated colleagues, psychiatrists may find it difficult to believe that the general public could be compassionate and accepting. In the same vein, many psychiatrists, from time to time, experience hostility from the rest of the medical community toward their specialty. Some psychiatrists are quite sensitive to real and imagined prejudice by their medical colleagues. With these therapists, the danger of identifying with the patient as a victim of an equally rejecting community is ever present.

Contact with the Community at Large

There are few ways a society can dramatically demonstrate acceptance of its mentally ill. Mental health professionals, as others, often generate conclusions from fairly fragmentary but vivid and memorable data. The many patients who successfully gain employment, the many mental health facilities erected without any stir from neighborhood associations, and other nondramatic developments are not brought to the attention of the psychiatrist. The large-scale support for mental health associations goes unnoticed. The question of how many other categories of illness attract such wide public participation is never asked. On the other hand, when a neighborhood association makes a fuss before a zoning board concerning a day-care center, few forget the unreasoning bitterness and anger. When a bigoted employer states that he "won't have any 'nuts' working for him," it is easy to forget the numerous employers reacting in understanding and sympathetic ways. Companies may arbitrarily and unreasonably refuse to employ individuals with mild cardiac conditions, but no one writes of the stigma of heart disease!

In summary then, it would appear that the psychiatrist's social status as protector of persecuted patients, his need to maintain a benign helpful stance in the face of hateful behaviors, the temptation to explain therapeutic failures as the fault of someone outside the therapeutic dyad, and the psychiatrist's own experiences as a minority group member may all combine to determine the tendency to view public attitudes toward mental illness as negative and rejecting. Further, it may be easy for the psychiatrist to combine the few dramatic incidents indicating negative attitudes, the conviction of patients that they are unwanted and alien to their society, the 'scientistic' and the antipsychiatric viewpoint of some colleagues in general medicine, and the reports of "closed ranks" into a dangerously distorted portfolio that his patients are stigmatized and rejected. Lemkau summarizes this tendency particularly well: "The conclusion that the public rejects the mentally ill, the hospitals and the people who man them . . . has become very extreme at times, so that one almost pictures the psychiatrist crying in his beer and wailing that nobody loves him. In that condition, I find him peculiarly unlovable, particularly when I am the psychiatrist involved" (P. Lemkau 1965, p. 7).

Consequences for Mental Health

The widespread belief in the "theory of rejection" has potential for reaching every area of mental health endeavor with subsequent unfortunate consequences. Certainly the belief that the public is generally hostile could lead the psychiatrist to isolate his practice to his private office and to overutilize hospitalization. Readily available neighborhood social and occupational resources may be ignored. Potential sources of support for the patient may be excluded from the treatment process. The thrust toward isolation might well tend to produce just the negative feelings that allegedly justify the isolation of the mental health care system from other social, medical, and educational systems. The community mental health movement was designed to deal with just such isolation. The continuing belief of mental health professionals that the population at large rejects the mentally ill may discourage one from community mental health programs. How can one simultaneously argue persuasively for halfway houses, home visiting and home care, day hospitalization, extensive outpatient-care programs, etc., while also arguing that patients will face rejection, derogation, and humiliation at the hands of society? This schizophrenic position may seriously impair efforts to press for psychiatric programs other than state hospitalization behind locked doors.

Furthermore, there may be a strong element of self-fulfilling prophecy in the myth of stigma and prejudice. In many ways, the expectation that prejudical attitudes will occur tends to make such attitudes acceptable. An unnecessary chasm may be produced, which separates mental health professionals from their medical colleagues and other sources of patient referral. This isolation tends to produce prejudice. Such belief has led many a therapist to isolate and insulate his practice from other social institutions in the community, thus reducing feedback about the actual parameters of his patient's social reality. In the same vein, many psychiatrists have tended to advise the patient to hide his illness from employers, fellow workers, neighbors, and even friends. Some have gone even further and have advised the patient to lie about his psychiatric history. Secrecy and deceitfulness, implicitly or explicitly approved by the therapist, can only have deleterious effects on the therapeutic relationship.

In the therapy situation itself, such belief may interfere with, or even impair, the therapist's ability to examine objectively the cause of his patient's maladaptation, dissatisfaction, and failure in the adjustment to his social role after hospitalization. This impairment would at best cloud the therapist's judgment of the reality or fantasy of the hostility in the patient's environment and the extent that the patient's behavior is responsible for the hostility. At worst, the therapist might join the patient in a paranoid folie à deux about society, thus making the patient's adaptation all but impossible.

The belief that stigma is attached to mental hospitalization is potentiálly harmful and dangerous. For many patients, early hospitalization is the treatment of choice. For others, hospitalization is one of the needed resources during the course of therapy. The consequences of belief in the stigma of hospitalization go beyond depriving many patients of the optimum mode of treatment. If avoidance of hospitalization becomes an irrational goal of the treatment, then the subsequent occurrence of hospitalization may be seen by the therapist as a failure of treatment. The least consequence of this conclusion would be the development of a corresponding feeling of failure in the patient.

The most significant implications of rejective public attitudes toward the mentally ill are found in the attribution of responsibility for the condition of mental institutions. The joint commission, in writing of mental hospitals, quoted one of the pioneers in opening the locked wards of the New York state hospitals, Robert C. Hunt: "The custodial culture within a state hospital is largely created by public pressure for security" (1961, p. 49). Subsequently the commission wrote:

> The literature on the status of our mental hospitals is monumental. . . . Most seems predicated on the assumption that if the plight—the shameful, dehumanized condition—of mentally sick people who populate the back wards of State Hospitals were sufficiently well exposed the public would rise in moral indignation. . . The assumption is ordinarily a valid one in a democracy . . . but something is missing in all this eloquence. . . . Why is it not correct to assume that public education regarding the facts about mental illness will stimulate action? . . . The care received by the mentally ill in the United States is the product of two great human forces, the desire to punish and to pity. . . . Obviously of the two forces punishment has exerted a greater force than pity. . . . The greater evidence of this . . . is that many hospitals for mental patients remain hospitals in name only. (1961, pp. 56 ff.)

It is impossible to avoid the conclusion that an almost primary responsibility for the atrocious conditions of many state institutions is being placed on public attitudes. Certainly it is true that state mental hospitals are neither built, administered, nor manned in a political and social vacuum. Nevertheless, it is unreasonable to assume that none of their "shameful, dehumanized conditions" are due at least sometimes, and at least in some part, to professional incompetence, financial inadequacy, and bureaucratic rigidity. As in the case of the individual therapist, public attitudes can be an extremely convenient scapegoat for the explanation of failure to maintain a medically adequate institution. Further, as with the individual therapist, it is easy to understand how a professional, daily facing frustration, personnel inadequacies, underbudgeting, impossible therapeutic conditions, and unrealistic expectations as to therapeutic outcome, may project his hostility onto a vaguely defined "public." It is even possible that for the realistic situational determinants of the role of "state mental hospital psychiatrist" to remain congruent with the professional role of "psychiatrist," the conceptualization of an extremely hostile and rejecting public is required.

Whether the assumption is that the patient needs to be protected from a hostile public or that the public needs protection from a dangerous patient, the barrier itself creates a vicious cycle of suspicion, fear, and distance. The very policies and practices of these hospitals may be the basis on which unfavorable public attitudes develop. The belief in the negative aspects of public attitudes toward the mentally ill may lead to removal of the patients from what is "bad" in the community without evaluating what is "good" about the community. The patient's healthy relationships may be disrupted along with those which are pathological. The very structure of the present-day state mental hospital is also decisive in forming some lingering negative public attitudes toward the mentally ill. It is paradoxical to keep patients under lock and key and then to try to convince the public that mental illness is like any other illness or that the mentally ill are no more violent, dangerous, or criminal than other people. What is the public to believe: the actions of the authority or its words?

The Theory's Appeal to Social Scientists

Belief in the social rejection of the mentally ill has had a significant effect in sociological theory, specifically the theory of social deviance. With few exceptions (Cohen 1959, Merton 1957, Parsons 1958), many who have written in this area have conceived of the mentally ill as prima facie simple social deviants (Clausen and Yarrow 1966, Scheff 1966, Dohrenwend and Chin-Shong 1967).

The empirical basis for the generalization has been the punitive rejection of the mentally ill by society. The reasoning is, essentially, that since the mentally ill are punitively sanctioned, therefore, they must be deviants. Occasionally the inference takes the reverse form, that is, since the mentally ill are deviants, they must, therefore, be socially rejected (Cumming and Cumming 1957). However, in whatever form, the idea of rejection provides the crucial empirical link between the equating of the social deviant and the mentally ill. By a simple extension the idea is carried further and mental illness becomes simply a form of deviant behavior (Sarbin and Mancuso 1970, Clausen and Yarrow 1966, Szasz 1961, Scheff 1966).

The idea derives further support from the fact that many mental illnesses manifest themselves as disturbances in interpersonal relations, or in bizarre or morally outrageous behavior and are without clear-cut origins. There is an attractive and even elegant simplicity in the conceptualization. At one stroke the difficult and confusing miscellany of psychiatric diagnostic categories is eliminated; etiological perplexities are at least partially resolved; and complex typologies of deviant behavior are avoided. Explicitly or implicitly the key criterion of deviance becomes social response. Those behaviors which are punitively sanctioned by society are considered deviant. Further, the hierarchial classification of deviant behavior typical of mental illness may be treated as an index of response to deviance. Studies have been reported where the differential response to case descriptions of the mentally ill among different social classes has been treated as a class measure of toleration of deviancy (Dohrenwend and Chin-Shong 1967).

However, there is a circular reinforcement in that the conceptualization of mental illness as social deviancy demands the existence of a public that is hostile and rejecting of the mentally ill. This may account for the selective bias in the perception of empirical data. There is some evidence that this has occurred. For example, in 1950 there were two opinion surveys of popular response to the mentally ill. One investigated the population of two small Canadian towns; the other, the population of Louisville, Kentucky. The investigators were of equal competence. The results were not radically dissimilar. The interpretations were. Woodward reported his study under the somewhat optimistic title, "Changing Ideas of Mental Illness and Its Treatment" (1951). The Cummings reported their findings under the less encouraging title *Closed Ranks* (1957). Woodward described his findings: "The change in a generation . . . should hearten sociologists, the social workers and the psychiatrists. This at least is the conclusion to be drawn from the research study about to be described" (p. 1). The Cummings concluded: "The community had . . . effectively closed ranks through apathy, withdrawal and hostility" (p. 199).

In virtually every investigation of public response to mental illness, the Cummings' study is cited; the Woodward study is rarely mentioned. In the joint commission's report the Cummings' findings are described. There is no mention of Woodward. In the massive text *A Comprehensive Textbook of Psychiatry*, a volume of considerable influence in forming the opinion of young psychiatrists, the article on sociology and psychiatry extensively describes the Cummings' investigation and interpretation. There is no mention of any alternative interpretation (Silverman 1967).

It would be frivolous to suggest that this selectivity of

emphasis represents willful bias or ignorance on the part of the sociological theorist. What is involved is the much deeper issue of the relationship between theory and research. The very elegance of the conceptualization of the mentally ill as simple social deviants provides a fruitful theoretical soil in which inference may flourish. Relatively limited findings can be linked directly to broad and significant sociological variables. By contrast what can be done with a finding that the mentally ill are socially acceptable? In the present state of social theory, such a positive finding has neither a theoretical nor an ideological relevance. It can only be reported as relatively isolated empirical data and will be treated as such. If perceived at all by theorists it will probably be regarded as an idiosyncratic exception, a sort of empirical sport, or else an attempt will be made to remold the finding into a form more acceptable to the theory. In a recent paper Sarbin and Mancuso described one such finding as "contradicting a chain of evidence," thus suggesting that it stands in isolation (1970). The "chain of evidence" on examination becomes in actuality a chain of inference. Their analysis of the Baltimore study's finding that 50 percent of a group of respondents "could imagine themselves as falling in love with someone who had been mentally ill" is reported as "only 50 percent."

What seems to happen when there is only one prevalent theory of the sociological role of the mentally ill is that findings which confirm that theory have a much greater relevance to a broader range of sociological issues than findings which do not. Consequently, confirmatory findings are cited much more frequently by theorists and interpreters in diverse fields than findings which contradict the theory. The result for the nonspecialist is the creation of a false illusion of empirical unaminity.

A priori assumption of the truth of the "theory of rejection" is appealing in other ways for the students of society. Some have made the implicit assumption that the prejudice toward the mentally ill is similar to prejudice against ethnic outgroups.

The assumption has even been explicitly noted (Chin-Shong 1968, Goffman 1963). The striking similarity between the statements about stereotypy, stigma, and rejection of the mentally ill on the one hand and the accounts of racial or ethnic prejudice on the other is unmistakable. Public attitudes toward ethnic outgroups have been examined, psychoanalyzed, deplored, and legalized. Some authors have found it tempting to conceptualize similarly the subculture of the mentally ill, with its implication of degradation and alienation. This temptation has been whetted by certain similarities. Many a former mental hospital patient is unemployed; some are introspective or depressed. Many are heavy users of drugs. Some employers would not hire a known former mental hospital patient. Many former mental hospital patients live at or below the poverty line. Some were poor to begin with, but a good many are bewildered and bitter *nouvaux pauvres,* their savings devoured by medical expenses, and their jobs lost through a prolonged illness or series of illnesses. Some families disavow their mentally ill member and treat him with a kind of totalitarian cruelty. The concept of social prejudice then may be easily employed if the "theory of rejection" is assumed as a given.

For some social theorists, abandoning the "theory of rejection" would be tantamount to abandoning a most fertile field of study, that is, the prejudice toward the mentally ill. Selective inattention to the empirical findings of recent major studies that little evidence could be found for stereotypy, stigma, or rejection of the mentally ill is, therefore, not surprising. The temptation for social scientists to invoke the specter of prejudice is only equaled by the absurdity of such a notion. Most studies about ethnic prejudice deal with attitudes of majority groups toward socially visible minorities distant from sources of community power. What is universally deplored is that the prejudices held by members of majority groups or powerful ingroups limit the freedom of achievement or well-being of the victims and influence them in a negative way. The mental patient has very little in common with the ethnic outgroup. He does not have similar social visibility. He does not necessarily belong to a group which is distant from sources of community power. Coming from a cross section of the population, he does not represent any particular educational, economic, or social class, or a minority culture. In fact, he may himself be a member of a powerful ingroup. The only common feature that the mental patient has with the ethnic outgroups is that of the segregation which is imposed on him when he is institutionalized or the degree of self-segregation which he imposes on himself because of his illness. The geographical segregation of the mentally ill person disappears when he is discharged from the mental hospital. The improvement or cure in his illness also brings to an end his self-imposed segregation. The active expectations that the mentally ill patient will return to his pre-illness position and conform to the institutionalized norm of his own particular group are very different from the attitudes of the power-holding majority toward the acculturation of minority or immigrant groups into long-established society. The absence of empirical evidence for prejudice toward the mentally ill, therefore, is hardly surprising. It would have been most surprising if it were otherwise. The public could hardly view the millions of mental patients and ex-mental patients as an alien race to which the average man will never belong.

Summary and Conclusion

Based on the viewpoint expressed here, one might reasonably assume that many reading this book will have difficulty accepting its conclusions. Challenging the conventional wisdom may lead to irritation and disbelief. If our speculations concerning the importance of the rejection theory are accurate, any empirical evidence demonstrating its incorrectness will be viewed with grave suspicion. Thus one can but "interpret the resistance." That has been the thrust of this chapter.

The experience of the mental health professional in his personal life, his training, his work with his patients, and his contact with professional colleagues and the community at large may all help to explain why a rejection theory would seem appealing to him. We ourselves have experienced such resistance in accepting our own data until it was apparent that in no way could the empirical findings be interpreted as confirmatory of the rejection hypothesis.

The consequences of such a tenacious belief in an unsupported hypothesis may be dismal. The expectations concerning public attitudes may border on the paranoid. Paranoid stances rarely produce fruitful collaboration in social systems. With such a stance, what shall one expect of the working alliance which must be forged between the mental health professional and the public? Thus the perilous consequences of the rejection theory seem as prevalent as its appeal.

In the social sciences as well the rejection hypothesis has its appeal and its consequences. Weighty hypotheses concerning prejudice, stigma, and social deviance rest on a "house-of-cards" theory of social rejection. Perhaps here, too, some revision would not be inappropriate.

Conclusion: Beyond the Data

The reflections that led to the writing of this book could have taken us in many directions. The choice of the modest goal of testing the "theory of rejection" permitted the employment of a research design to which the apparatus of scientific inquiry could be applied. Our task was completed at the conclusion of chapter 8. The main purpose of this work was to test by survey data the following propositions:

1. That the public recognizes only the paranoid schizophrenic as mentally ill
2. That the public is unwilling to consider the mentally ill as "sick" or in need of medical care
3. That the public stereotypes the mentally ill and mental illness
4. That the public isolates the mentally ill by denying personal contact with them and insisting on institutionalization
5. That the public wants such institutionalization to be punitive or custodial in nature
6. That the public resists the return of the labeled mentally ill to conventional social roles by maintaining maximum social distance from them

These propositions were tested in various forms. Since 1960, there has been no substantial body of data that unequivocally supports any of the above propositions. Most reported findings contradict them. Therefore, their continued utilization as a basis for public policy, as a factor in social psychiatry, and as a premise in sociological theory is empirically unwarranted.

In chapter 9 we briefly described some observations about recent changes in the treatment of the mentally ill and how the public reacted to these changes. In chapter 10 we speculated on the appeal of and some of the consequences of the belief in the "theory of rejection," the attraction of which is attested to by the scant attention paid to the voluminous contradictory evidence in the literature. The overwhelming cumulative evidence presented in this volume may also stand in isolation and the theoretical significance of these data lost unless a theoretically integrated interpretation can be made. The meaning of these findings will remain ambiguous if they are not examined in the context of certain kinds of propositions. These propositions or hypotheses are needed to clarify the relationship between the data and the conclusions. In this chapter we wish to speculate beyond the limits of the data in search of logical arguments related to the practice of social psychiatry and to an alternative theory of social response to mental illness compatible with the larger and traditional body of sociological theory.

Social Deviance and Group Solidarity

The most widely respected sociological theory of punishment is Durkheim's (1933). Although stated in various forms, the central proposition is that the social function of punishment is the symbolic affirmation of group solidarity. Deviancy is punished not to deter deviant behavior but so that the social group may continuously affirm its cohesion. In logical structure this is not widely different from the psychoanalytic viewpoint that would see in the punishment of others the strengthening of repression in self. If Durkheim's concept of the function of punishment is valid and if the data showing the acceptance of the former mentally ill are credited, then it must follow that in contemporary society the social perceptions of the behavior of the mentally ill—the symptoms of many mental illnesses—are no longer perceived as threats to social cohesion.

It is questionable whether the deviant behavior of those defined as mentally ill ever constitutes a true threat to social cohesion. So long as the behavior is first defined as truly "ill" by a socially sanctioned professional expert, that is, the physician, the behavior sets no new norms, creates no new precedents. It is when hysterical behavior is socially sanctioned, accepted, and rewarded, as in the Salem witchcraft trials, that the behavior may prove contagious and threatening.

In chapters 6 and 8 data were presented showing that the UAW members were virtually unanimous in their willingness to accept a former mental patient as a workmate. The inference is that a past history of mental illness is not considered threatening in the context of their work experience.

A great deal is known about the work situation of these men. In Appendix D it is pointed out that they have been at the same job for an average of over thirteen years, that their working situation is not so much the result of individual achievement as it is due to the process of collective bargaining, and that they enjoy a somewhat higher family income and greater job stability than their immediate neighbors. The key focus of the union is on job security, wages, and hours. Job security is a vital element in the way of life of these workers. In practice this means that layoffs and rehiring must be strictly in terms of seniority. A man may not be removed from his job out of the order of seniority save for carefully stipulated and zealously restricted reasons. Wildcat strikes have occurred merely on the rumor of such a possibility. The personal characteristics of a worker are definitely not permissible reasons for violating the job-security provisions of the union contract.

Almost all of these men work on an assembly line. They do not work with so much as alongside their fellow workers. Social interaction is optional. Group cohesion and social solidarity are expressed in union elections, in the unconditional compliance with a strike vote, and in ceasing work when ordered to do so by a shop steward.

In the absence of theoretical preconceptions it is impossible to anticipate from such a work context any rejection of a worker who has been mentally ill. When the extensive contact this population has had with mental illness and the provision of prepaid inpatient and outpatient psychiatric care in the labor contract are added to this definition of the work situation, the expectation of the rejection of a fellow worker simply because he has been mentally ill borders on the fatuous. It is not a question of the increasing or decreasing acceptance of the mentally ill; it is that the characteristics involved in having been mentally ill are simply irrelevant. The institutionalized expectations and the institutionalized expression of group cohesion are not threatened by the individual member's symptoms of mental illness. These symptoms do not exist in the same domain of perception. One is more likely to produce a wildcat strike by firing a man whom a doctor says is mentally ill than by hiring such a man.

The fact that a majority of this population would not object to having one of their children marry a former mental patient was established (chapters 6 and 8). In chapter 8 it was pointed out that the nature of this acceptance is provisional, that is, having been mentally ill does not in and of itself preclude the possibility of an individual becoming a member of one of these working-class families by marriage. Something is known of the structure of these families. As stated in Appendix D, they are almost all nuclear families—parents and dependent children. Few sons-in-law and daughters-in-law are found in the households. Evidently in this population marriage means the setting up of independent households with future relationships primarily on a voluntary basis. The impression given by conventional literature is that in contemporary society marriage choice is largely left to the individual. Consequently, opposing an offspring's selection of a marriage partner might well mean terminating whatever residual parental relationship is left after marriage, as well as failing to conform to the sentimentalized cultural goal of freedom of mate selection. To this highly job-oriented population, the employment prospects of a future in-law might well be of greater significance than his personal characteristics.

One might well expect that in such a situational context and without a priori bias, past mental illness would not be a very important factor in opposing a marriage choice. As with the work situation, the affirmation of family cohesion and solidarity or of the family's social status is not achieved by the rejection or punishment of the particular characteristics involved in severe mental illness. Probably of greater concern is the capacity for mutual economic assistance. Failure to conform on this level is much more likely to be punitively sanctioned.

All of the foregoing have been derived from the social characteristics of the UAW population of Baltimore. Logically, however, the interpretations should be applicable to any population with similar characteristics. In brief, in populations that work and live as this population does, it is no longer necessary—if indeed it ever was—to punish a person's symptoms of mental illness as a means of maintaining social order. In more sociological terms, the institutionalized patterns of social cohesion and group solidarity are neither threatened by, nor do they rest on, the presence or absence of symptoms of mental illness.

What is being argued has been stated explicitly by Merton, Broom, and Cottrell (1959), Parsons (1958, ch. 7), and Cohen (1959). Deviancy is not to be defined by the characteristics of the social behavior concerned but in terms of the institutional structure and cultural milieu in which it occurs. Some mental disorders among some populations at some times have undoubtedly been defined as socially deviant. Others, such as types of compulsive conformity, probably never have been. Therefore, the acceptance or rejection (punishment) of the mentally ill by any given population at any given time is not to be understood in terms of the general toleration of deviancy but in terms of the values and specific institutional structures of that population and the particular symptoms of the specific illness under discussion. All that the present data have shown is that the general referent of "having been in a mental hospital" for a particular kind of industrial working-class population does not in and of itself conjure up fantasied threats to group cohesion sufficient to warrant rejection.

Socioeconomic Issues in State Hospitalization

For some decades in the United States the diagnosis of a mental illness for a poor person was usually followed by involuntary hospitalization in a prisonlike institution remote from the victim's community. Yet this had not always been the picture. The mass hospitalization of the mentally ill began as part of a great wave of humanitarian reform appearing in the United States in the post-Civil War period. Its original purpose was to protect the indigent mentally ill from economic and social exploitation. To this day state mental hospital systems and welfare systems are inextricably intertwined in many states. Some state laws dealing with the commitment process speak of "paupers"; others, of "foreign paupers." It is interesting to note that although the motivation for the rescue from social and economic serfdom of the indigent mentally ill was moral, it occurred at about the same historical period that burgeoning American capitalism discovered that human slavery was no longer a viable economic institution.

Originally many state hospitals were not prisonlike custodial institutions, but became so with a tremendous increase in the number of patients without a corresponding increase in size and staff. The sharp rise in the number of patients was due to population growth; furthermore the huge influx of immigrants between 1890 and 1914 meant that an increasing proportion of the inmates was culturally and ethnically alien to the staff and the community. In urbanized states the large migration of blacks to the cities and their subsequent addition to the mental hospital population added a further complication.

Hospitalization was probably always a class-biased process. The poorest members of the population had the highest probability of being hospitalized for mental illness, and the poorest mentally ill had the best chance of being sent to the qualitatively poorest hospitals. Traces of what was probably once a much more widespread pattern of class-biased hospitalization are still to be found. The Hollingshead and Redlich studies have shown a distinct class bias in the recommendation for hospital versus nonhospital treatment of the mentally ill (1958). Thus at one point in time to be mentally ill meant to be imprisoned under dehumanizing conditions with what were considered the dregs of society—blacks, Italians, Eastern Europeans—and thus to suffer an almost total loss of social status, that is, to be stigmatized.

The reasons offered for this barbarism were almost always couched in terms of the characteristics of the patients rather than the characteristics of the institutions. Patients were locked up and treated inhumanly because they were allegedly dangerous and barely human. In time this justification developed many of the characteristics of a self-fulfilling prophecy.

The facts of the case concerning the conditions of treatment are not in dispute (Beers 1908, Deutsch 1949). What is in dispute is whether these individuals were treated in this manner because they were labeled mentally ill or whether they were treated in this manner because they were the indigent ill from the working class and of unacceptable ethnic origin. Were the characteristics that distinguished the mentally ill from the rest of society the characteristics of their diseases or was it their longevity—even under atrocious conditions—coupled with the frequently institutionally induced chronicity of their illnesses until they came to occupy more than one-half of all the hospital beds in the United States? Just how different was their treatment at the time from the treatment of the indigent ill in the nursing homes, the institutions for the retarded, hospitals for chronically ill, terminal facilities, homes for the indigent aged, and institutions for grossly handicapped? Just how different is such care today?

The testing of the hypothesis that there was and probably is no significant difference between the custodial care of the indigent chronically ill and the indigent, or medically indigent, mentally ill is beyond the scope of this work. However, if the hypothesis could be substantiated, some interesting ideological issues would be raised. It would mean in effect that the emphasis on the special social nature of mental illness, making it distinct from other illnesses, has a function of masking the common reality problem of the economics of humanely caring for the chronically ill in a success- and property-oriented society. This is analogous to the function of racism in the working class. By dividing common interest, racism frustrates common action and common solution to common problems.

This socioeconomic hypothesis may help explain differential attitudes toward those who seek psychoanalysis and those who go to state hospitals. Shifts in attitudes since the advent of insurance coverage for mental illness and the development of mental health centers may be further evidence in support of this hypothesis.

Attitudes Toward Illness

Most of the studies of popular attitudes toward mental illness have assumed explicitly or implicitly that there must necessarily be a difference in attitudes toward those illnesses termed "mental" and those termed "physical." There is no factual basis for this assumption in the literature. The undesirable behaviors associated with some mental illnesses are cited as reason for the public's differential attitude toward mental and physical illnesses. Violently assaultive symptoms of catatonic excitement do not allow for close social interaction. Equally, however, when an individual suffers from a ruptured appendix and severe peritonitis ensues, the surgical drains placed through the abdominal wall yield a characteristically unpleasant odor that might cause many persons to avoid sharing a room with him. The fact that in the one case the motive may be physical fear and in the other nausea does not alter either the attitudinal or behavioral result of avoidance. If both these patients were expected to retain their symptoms for years, they might eventually be regarded as afflicted with stigmatizing illnesses. Before the days of well-fitting colostomy bags, one of the functions of colostomy clubs was to help individuals deal with such interpersonal problems.

Another organic illness which has been associated with "prejudice" is epilepsy. Patients suffering from epileptic seizures engage in a series of behaviors which may be distressing and upsetting to onlookers. Epileptics have faced discriminatory treatment in the past and they continue to face difficulty gaining certain types of employment because of fear that they may fall into machinery or be subject to other accidents and dangers. One can draw many parallels back and forth between other so-called "physical" and "mental" illnesses in similar terms.

In years gone by, the behaviors associated with chronic mental illness were often most disruptive and upsetting. With somatic treatments such as chemotherapy and shock therapy, more effective inpatient treatment, group and individual psychotherapy, and better follow-up care, the behaviors have been ameliorated. This may explain improving public attitudes. However, the association of mental illness with disruptive behavior may still produce high social distance.

For some time now, a group of physical illnesses such as asthma, peptic ulcer, colitis, migraine headaches, hypertension, etc., have been referred to as "psychosomatic illnesses." The psychosocial causes contributing to these illnesses have been emphasized. The more recent trend in psychosomatic medicine has been to focus on the psychological and social events which markedly influence the course of such illnesses as tuberculosis, diabetes, susceptibility to viral infections, etc. Even more impressive has been the new evidence to indicate organic mediators and factors in conditions previously classified as "mental illness." Research in the bioamines, the influence of the limbic system, methyl doners, etc., has initiated the process of tracing out the organic factors related to depressive illnesses, manic-depressive psychoses, and schizophrenia. This current research is but a continuation of a long-standing trend to understand the psychological, the social, and the organic components in disease. Less than a century ago, paretic patients were viewed as suffering from a mental illness similar in nature to schizophrenia. The discovery of the relationship of the treponema pallidum, tertiary syphilis, and paresis made this condition as organic as pneumonia, cancer, or any other physical illness. It is ironic indeed that at a time when physicians are more and more coming to understand the relationship between the psychological and the physical that some should insist upon classifying mental illness as a product of social deviancy unrelated to other medical illnesses.

In summary then the public attitudes toward various mental illnesses should be seen as part of a unified theory of illness, and the specific variables determining attitudes toward mental illness identical with those determining attitudes toward any illness. This hypothesis can only be tested by examining attitudes toward specific symptom clusters rather than global concepts like "mental illness." One must be particularly cautious when drawing conclusions about emotional symptoms in the absence of organic "control" symptoms. We postulate that upsetting behavior will provoke avoidance response irrespective of etiology or presumed pathogenesis. This need *not* be a homeostatic mechanism to protect the social organism against threat. These are individual defenses against noxious stimuli or psychologically distressing events and may be expected to vary in intensity and manifestation according to the stimuli and characteristics of the individual involved.

The Sick Role

The societal consensus that the mentally ill are sick and in need of medical care supports the hypothesis that the same variables that affect the social responses toward all illnesses affect the social responses to mental illness. Attitudes are different toward an acute infectious process that is self-limited and a chronically draining tuberculosis sinus tract. Upsetting facial disfigurement would create different feelings than a readily remedial fracture. The acute disturbance of a febrile delirium apparently brings down no stigma. The expectation that the delirium will go on for twenty years would yield a very different reaction. We would thus speculate that so-called "prejudice" toward an illness would correlate highly with the expectation that the condition is likely to recur and produce troubling behavior. The sociological frame of reference here is the "sick role." This concept was formalized by Parsons (1958) and has been described in chapter 2 of this book. As the term implies, the sick role is an interactional concept. It does not merely specify the expected behavior involved in the status of being sick, but the expected responses of those interacting with the sick person. Gordon, through intensive empirical study of public response to a variety of physical illnesses and handicaps, has brought Parson's concept to a higher level of refinement and specificity. Gordon writes: "For all socio-economic groups the major factor in defining someone as sick appears to be the prognosis" (1966, p. 99). By this he means the difference between an uncertain or worsening prognosis and a known nonserious one.

Gordon found that responses to the sick role were not continuous scalable variables but tended to cluster around two unrelated sets of expectations. The first, more typical of the acute short-term illness with time-limited incapacity, was essentially the set of expectations postulated by Parsons—the sick role. The second was more typical of non-life-threatening illnesses with persistent symptomatology and known prognosis, leading to the impaired role. In the first role, the person is insulated and protected from the demands of normal life. In the impaired role, the person is encouraged, within the limits of his condition, to maintain normal activities and involvement.

Overwhelmingly the populations studied in the 1960s believed that mental illness was curable with "proper treatment." However, these responses were made in terms of the global concept "mental illness" by a public that was also aware of the great variety of illnesses and behaviors that could be included under such a rubric. The long-standing, often unwarranted, prognostic pessimism which afflicted psychiatry throughout the nineteenth and much of this century should be borne in mind when examining the earlier findings, as well as the present minority who hold negative attitudes toward the mentally ill. Public attitudes have not developed in a vacuum. These considerations lead to the hypothesis that a closer examination of specific symptom clusters of psychiatric illnesses would reveal both the sick role and the impaired role as dimensions of social response. If this hypothesis is valid, it would be possible to have a differential attitudinal social distance toward each role. It could also imply that a key factor in improving public attitudes is not only the public's capacity to differentiate between different mental illnesses but the recognition that for some mental illnesses recovery can be complete.

Most of the studies of attitudes toward the mentally ill, including our own, used a *recovered* mental patient as a referent. Responses must, at least in part, have been shaped by attitudes about "recovery." Modern chemotherapy has resulted in impressive advances in the control of schizophrenia and manic-depressive disease. Psychotherapy in all its forms is more available to the public. Changes in public reactions to the "recovered mental patient" since 1950 may simply reflect increased public awareness of such progress.

A different aspect of chronicity is related to disorders which follow frustratingly remittent or uncertain courses. Repeated exacerbations of distressing symptoms and behaviors may leave family and acquaintances realistically negative about the possibility for interpersonal closeness. Anger and derision may be directed at treating sources as the only safe target for the intense dysphoric affect induced by these conditions. This description is based primarily on experience in a liaison service working with patients with chronic collagen diseases, chronic infections, chronic cardiovascular disease, etc. The description is equally applicable to some chronic mental illnesses. The characteristics attributed to the public views of mental illness may relate to the type of chronicity of *some* of the disorders rather than all mental illnesses.

If the hypothesis is valid, what has really been studied is not so much the increased willingness of the public to permit the mental patient to adopt the sick role as the increased willingness of the public to let him out of that role. We would postulate that one of the important variables affecting the sick role in various illness conditions is the mode and possibility of egress from the sick role imposed by the illness and the treatment. For those mental illnesses where the only egress from the sick role is through the impaired role we would predict a higher attitudinal social distance in the more intimate social relationships. We would further postulate that the more limited resources of lower socioeconomic groups to support such impaired members would lead to an inverse relationship between socioeconomic status and the degree of impairment on the one hand, and negative attitudes on the other.

In conclusion, it should be emphasized that the social role accorded the chronically impaired deserves future study. Parsons's formulation of the sick role, as Gordon has indicated, is not necessarily transferable to the chronically impaired. Issues of chronic dependency may be much harder to accept than more limited dependent stances. In a culture which continues to place a high value on self-reliance, independence, self-sufficiency, and acquisitiveness, those who need help over a long time span are thrown into difficult roles. If the sick role is premised on cooperation and egocentric self-indulgence to achieve recovery, what happens in the event that recovery is unattainable?

Attitudes of Health Professionals

Treatment approaches utilized in an illness have a significant role in public attitudes. When patients are placed in straitjackets, when they are locked in grim bastions behind bars, when they are carried off against their will by men in white suits, an onlooker might conclude that the patient was capable of some very upsetting behaviors. Phillips's research would tend to confirm this hypothesis in that the same conditions were differentially regarded depending upon the treatment source. In his study, the most "prejudice" emerged when the treatment source was a state hospital (Phillips 1963).

In contrast, strongly expressed beliefs by psychiatrists that psychiatric patients can be treated in mental health centers in their communities, that they can be expected to remain at work, and that they can recover quickly may have far more impact than any publicity campaigns for mental health. Indeed the Star findings in 1950 may have been an accurate portrayal of the viewpoints influenced by the state-care systems of the thirties and forties. More recent findings may reflect the influence of both the psychopharmacology and community-psychiatry revolutions.

On the other hand, if not based on social reality, the emphasis on the unique nature of the social response to the mentally ill as distinct from those with other illnesses functions to hinder changes in the direction of community, outpatient, and home treatment. If the mentally ill are so rejected and deviant that they cannot be treated in the community then they must be treated in institutions. If they are treated in institutions, this becomes proof that the community, in fact, rejects them.

This in turn reinforces any rejective community attitudes and completes the cycle of rejection, isolation, and insulation of the mentally ill.

It is asserted—admittedly without documentation—that the prevalent professional belief in the overwhelming social rejection of the mentally ill is probably the largest single barrier to the implementation of rationally financed, effective, comprehensive care of the mentally ill. Care which is solely based on the patients' needs might be hospital based, community based, home based, or outpatient based. Technically, few barriers remain to this type of comprehensive treatment for many of the illnesses termed "mental." At the UAW clinic, patients with process schizophrenia have been maintained for four years at home and on the job without hospitalization at a cost of $400 per year by means of judicious medication and supportive psychotherapy. This prepaid, exclusively working-class clinic has been neither swamped by malingerers—a dire prediction of some—nor shunned because of the alleged stigmatization attendant on psychiatric treatment. Similar experiences are widely reported.

The Theory of Acceptance

At the heart of the professional controversy over the nature of social response to the mentally ill lies the question: Are they considered "sick" or "deviant"? In the one case it is logical to expect social response to be the same as that accorded any victim of illness; in the other, punitive social sanction would be the expectation.

Erickson has commented on deviance as follows: "Sociologically, then, the critical variable in the study of deviance is the social audience rather than the individual person, since it is the audience which eventually decides whether or not any given action or actions will become a visible case of deviance" (1962, p. 308). Similarly, Becker states that "deviant behavior is behavior that people so label" (1963, p. 9).

In the UAW study more than 90 percent of the "audience" label the mentally ill as "sick." Every study reporting responses to similar questions has obtained approximately the same results (chapter 5). The UAW population is virtually unanimous in its willingness to accept a former mental patient as a workmate. A majority of this population would not object to having one of their children marry a former mental patient. These are hardly the responses that a group typically offers to social deviance. Goffman states: "The sick can be free, then, to be deviators precisely because their deviations can be fully discounted, leading to no re-identification; their special situation demonstrates that they are anything but deviants in the common understanding of that term" (1963, p. 141).

Accordingly, by the standards of the "labeling theory" cited above, the data reviewed in this work (chapters 5, 6, 7) should put an end to the sick-role-versus-deviance controversy among professionals, at least as it applies to unspecified and undescribed "mental illness." The labeling theorists may not continue calling the mentally ill deviants unless they choose to abandon their theoretical stance. What might still remain a subject for fruitful empirical inquiry, if not sweeping theoretical generalization, is popular response to specific clusters of symptoms by specific populations under specific circumstances.

The first question about the validity of the "sick role" has now been answered. The public refuses to label the mentally ill as deviant and demands the privileges and the rights of the sick role for them. Ultimate clarification, however, must depend upon the solution of the second question, now to be considered: How is public unanimity possible in the presence of professional dichotomy of opinion, continued existence of many prisonlike state hospitals, continued practice of judicial commitment, negative stereotypes of the mentally ill presented by the mass communication media, and the continued existence of many disruptive and distressing symptoms of mental illness?

Having questioned the "theory of rejection," we feel obliged also to explore the public reasons for the acceptance of the mentally ill. The evaluation of the reasons for public insistence on seeing the mentally ill in the same light as the physically ill is so vital a point in integrating these data that one cannot overlook it without misapprehending the meaning of all these findings.

Hence the question must be reversed. Instead of asking why the mentally ill are stigmatized and rejected, the question becomes: Why are the mentally ill accepted, and why is there such consensus among the public for granting the mentally ill the sick role?

The analytical properties of the members of the UAW audience described earlier help explain the unanimity with which they are willing to accord the benefits and privileges of a medically approved "sick role" to the mentally ill. These UAW members are urban industrial workers, living in a nuclear-family structure where social status is completely dependent on job security. This security is defined in group terms—the union. They lack the security of possessing an ongoing tradition or of being part of extended families. They lack any material continuity with the past (little evidence was found of family silver, heirlooms, etc., in the home). Their almost total dependence on the plant, around which they live, would make it conceivable that if the plant moved to another area most of these workers, if given a choice, would follow the plant rather than remain and seek other employment. Thus the consensus, by refusing to label the mentally ill as deviant, serves a valuable social function.

For this population, labeling the mentally ill members as deviant, with all that this labeling implies in terms of punitive sanction and rejection, is incompatible with the need for social cohesion. When 85 percent admit to knowing someone who has been mentally ill and 57 percent identify this person as a family member or close friend, attachment of the stigma and the label of deviance to the mentally ill would be a devastating blow to the solidarity of the group.

It is, therefore, not surprising that they choose to perceive psychiatric symptoms in a medical framework, that is, as illness. Associated with this frame of reference is the assumption of sympathy and the suspension of moral judgment. Included is the enlistment of prestigious scientific methods to return the individual to health.

If this population were to label the mentally ill as deviant, with all that this entails, its own social relations would become even more tenuous. The concept of the "sick role" rests on the fundamental acceptance of a bargaining process by which humans ensure that their own incapacitation, or that of those close to them, receives sympathy and assistance rather than sanction by extending reciprocal sympathy and assistance to the affliction of others. The fundamental social process by which these individuals agree to the rules of bargaining and negotiation in determining their work situation is simply extended when the physician or mental health professional is given the role of arbiter of illness. This constitutes one of the basic means for the maintenance of predictable social responses in others and toward others, thus significantly reducing the hazards and uncertainties of their lives.

The demand for the inclusion of mental illness in the comprehensive health-insurance coverage originated with the union—not with management or with the medical community. This demand is further evidence of the high positive value the group places on the classification of mental illness as a medical problem.

All of the above inferences have been derived from the social characteristics of the UAW population of Baltimore. Logically, however, the interpretation should be applicable to any population with similar characteristics. The similarity in response reported in all the major studies of the 1960s suggest that broader generalizations are possible.

In an industrialized society many people simply lack the power to control their own destinies individually. Sources of dependency gratification which could provide such power are minimal. Being dependent on the rules of others, these people need to define as few deviant behaviors as possible in order to least endanger their own security and the security of those close to them. They seek the most inclusive definition of the "sick role."

The foregoing section sketches a theory of acceptance. It is neither the complete word on the subject nor the sole possible interpretation of all the data. What it does posit is that once universal vulnerability to an impairing condition, be it physical or mental, is perceived by members of a society, its conception as deviance becomes untenable within that society. It would lead us too far astray here to examine the soundness of this basic assumption. Let it suffice to crystalize its nature.

Social scientists and mental health professionals might usefully close ranks in pursuit of the complex combined social, medical, and psychological models required to understand both mental illness and the different responses it evokes. The time has come to write a belated epitaph to the "theory of rejection."

Appendices

Bibliography

Index

Partial Questionnaire of the Baltimore Study

1. Here is a list of some diseases. I'd like to know which you think would be the worst one for a person to have? Which would you say is the next worst? The next?

	First Choice	*Second Choice*	*Third Choice*	*Fourth Choice*	*Fifth Choice*
Cancer	*67.9%*	*21.3%*	*5.0%*	*2.1%*	*0.5%*
Heart disease	*15.8*	*39.7*	*27.4*	*8.7*	*5.2*
Tuberculosis	*5.0*	*14.4*	*26.1*	*28.2*	*22.6*
Mental illness	*22.6*	*21.0*	*24.3*	*24.4*	*13.7*
Diabetes	*1.5*	*9.9*	*19.0*	*27.7*	*39.4*

2. Now I'd like to describe a certain kind of person and ask you a few questions about her. She is a young woman in her twenties . . . let's call her Betty Smith. She has never had a job, and she doesn't seem to want to go and look for one. She is a very quiet girl, she doesn't talk much to anyone—even to her own family—and she acts like she is afraid of people, especially young men her own age. She won't go out with anyone and whenever someone comes to visit her family, she stays in her own room until they leave. She just stays by herself and daydreams all the time and shows no interest in anything or anybody.

1. Have you ever known anyone who acted like this?

Yes	*20%*
No	*79*
DK & NA	*1*

2. Would you say there is anything wrong with the young woman I told you about or not?

Something wrong (ASK "3")	*90%*
Nothing wrong (SKIP TO "6")	*8*
DK & NA (ASK "6")	*2*

3. Would you say this woman—Betty Smith—has some kind of mental illness—a sickness of the mind—or not?

Has (ASK "4")	*78%*
Has not (SKIP TO "6")	*10*
DK & NA (SKIP TO "6")	*4*

4. Would you say that the mental illness she has is a serious one or not?

Serious	*45%*
Not serious	*30*
DK & NA	*4*

5. Do you think this illness can be cured or not?

Can be cured	*72%*
Cannot be cured	*2*
DK & NA	*4*

6. Do you think this girl should see a doctor or not?

Should see doctor	*93%*
Should not	*5*
DK & NA	*2*

3. Now about Bill Williams. He never seems to be able to hold a job very long because he drinks so much. Whenever he has money in his pocket he goes on a spree; he stays out till all hours drinking and never seems to care about what happens to his wife and children. Sometimes he feels very bad about the way he treats his family; he begs his wife to forgive him and promises to stop drinking, but he always goes off again.

1. Have you ever known anyone who acted like this?

Yes	*55%*
No	*44*
DK & NA	*1*

2. Would you say there is anything wrong with the man I told you about or not?

Something wrong (ASK "3")	*88%*
Nothing wrong (SKIP TO "6")	*10*
DK & NA (ASK "3")	*2*

3. Would you say this man—Bill Williams—has some kind of mental illness—a sickness of the mind—or not?

Has (ASK "4")	*62%*
Has not (SKIP TO "6")	*24*
DK & NA (SKIP TO "6")	*5*

4. Would you say that the mental illness he has is a serious one or not?

Serious	*44%*
Not serious	*16*
DK & NA	*2*

5. Do you think this illness can be cured or not?

Can be cured	*56%*
Cannot be cured	*2*
DK & NA	*4*

6. Do you think this man should see a doctor or not?

Should see doctor	*84%*
Should not	*12*
DK & NA	*4*

4. Now here's a man—let's call him Frank Jones—who is very suspicious; he doesn't trust anybody, and he's sure that everybody is against him. Sometimes he thinks that people he sees on the street are talking about him or following him around. A couple of times, now, he has beaten up men who didn't even know him because he thought they were plotting against him. The other night he began to curse his wife terribly; then he hit her and threatened to kill her because, he said, she was working against him, too, just like everybody else.

1. Have you ever known anyone who acted like this?

Yes	*26%*
No	*74*
DK & NA	—

2. Would you say there is anything wrong with the man I told you about or not?

Something wrong (ASK *"3"*)	*95%*
Nothing wrong (SKIP TO *"6"*)	*4*
DK & NA (ASK *"3"*)	*1*

3. Would you say this man—Frank Jones—has some kind of mental illness—a sickness of the mind—or not?

Has (ASK *"4"*)	*91%*
Has not (SKIP TO *"6"*)	*3*
DK & NA (SKIP TO *"6"*)	*2*

4. Would you say that the mental illness he has is a serious one or not?

Serious	*78%*

Not serious	*12%*
DK & NA	*2*

5. Do you think this illness can be cured or not?

Can be cured	*79%*
Cannot be cured	*2*
DK & NA	*11*

6. Do you think this man should see a doctor or not?

Should see a doctor	*95%*
Should not	*3*
DK & NA	*2*

7. Here is a list of statements that are sometimes made about people who have been mentally ill. Some people agree with them and some disagree. What do you think about each statement? Do you agree?

Well, would you say that you agree with it more than you disagree, are more in agreement with it, *or* more in disagreement with it?

	Agree	*Disagree*	*DK & NA*
1. We should strongly discourage our children from marrying anyone who has been mentally ill.	*49%*	*46%*	*5%*
2. I can imagine myself falling in love with a person who had been mentally ill.	*51*	*44*	*5*
3. I would be willing to room with someone who had been a patient in a mental hospital.	*50*	*45*	*5*
4. I *wouldn't* hesitate to work with someone who had been mentally ill.	*81*	*17*	*2*
5. If I could do the job and the pay were right, I wouldn't mind working in a mental hospital.	*68*	*30*	*2*

8.1. Have you ever known anyone who was in a hospital because of mental illness?

Yes	*63%*

No (SKIP TO "16")	36%
DK & NA (SKIP TO "16")	1

2. How many have you known?

Just one (ASK "9-1")	25%
Two (ASK "9-2")	17
Three (ASK "9-2")	9
Four (ASK "9-2")	3
More than four (ASK "9-2")	9

9.1. Was this a relative, close friend, or someone you didn't know very well?

2. Of the people you knew who were in a mental hospital, pick the one you knew best. Was this person a member of your immediate family, some other relative, close friend or an acquaintance?

Respondent	1%
Immediate family	9
Other relative	12
Close friend	14
Acquaintance	25
Other (SPECIFY)	2
Won't say	—

3. In what year did this person go to the hospital?

1960	2%
1959	4
1958	5
1957	4
1956	3
1951-1955	14
1946-1950	10
1940-1945	7
Before 1940	10
DK & NA	5

4. Was this the only time this person went to the hospital for mental illness or were there more times? How many?

Yes	40%
No	9
Two	5
Three	3
Four	—
Five or more	1
DK & NA	5

12. Now here is something you might find interesting. . . . Something about people with mental illness is written on each of these cards. I'd like you to read *all* of these cards carefully and then, *after* you have read them all, put the cards you agree with on one side and the cards you *disagree* with on the other.

	Agree	*Disagree*	*DK & NA*
1. Everyone who has a mental illness should be placed in a mental hospital.	40%	57%	3%
2. Almost all persons who have a mental illness are dangerous.	22	74	4
3. Every mental hospital should be surrounded by a high fence and guards.	35	62	3
4. The best way to handle people in mental hospitals is to keep them behind locked doors.	18	77	5
5. There are many different kinds of mental illnesses.	92	5	3
6. All people with the same mental illness act in the same way.	11	83	6
7. People who have *some* kinds of mental illness can be taken care of at home.	84	12	3
8. Sometimes it is better for a person with a mental illness to live with his or her family instead of being in a mental hospital.	74	20	5
9. If someone living in the same family with me became mentally ill, I would certainly try to take care of them at home, *if* the doctor thought it wouldn't do any harm.	83	13	4

10. People who have been in a state mental hospital are no more likely to commit crimes than people who have never been in a state mental hospital.	*59%*	*32%*	*9%*

13. Now here are some real life situations. . . . Let's call these people the Joneses. Mary Jones is about 20 years old, single, and lives with her father, mother and younger brother. She's pretty, had a good enough job and always seemed to get along with everyone. Lately, though, she has had to stop working. She says she can't seem to keep her mind on anything anymore. She was always very quick but *now* whenever she has to read anything, she has to read it over two or three times before she can understand it. She doesn't seem to want to eat and she is losing weight. She doesn't care much how she looks anymore and often she doesn't even bother to get dressed or comb her hair. She's always tired and just doesn't want to do anything. She told her mother that "life just doesn't seem to be worth living anymore."

The doctor told her father and mother that he could arrange for Mary to go to a state mental hospital where a special doctor and nurse would try and make her better in a few weeks *or* that Mr. and Mrs. Jones could keep her at home and that he would arrange for a special doctor and nurse to come and see her at home from time to time and try and make her better in a few weeks. Either way the cost would be about the same. What should Mr. and Mrs. Jones do? Should they send Mary to the mental hospital *or* should they keep her at home?

Send to hospital	*40%*
Take care of at home	*56*
Depends	*2*
DK & NA	*2*

What makes you say that?

Change of environment desirable	*17%*
Quality of hospital care better	*31*
Quantity of hospital care better	*12*
Moral obligation to keep at home	—
Violence and custody handled better in hospital	*4*
Wife suffers	*1*
Family suffers	*1*
Tender loving care	*1*
Find self in mental hospital awful	—

14. Now here's another family story . . . about people in Baltimore. Mr. and Mrs. Walker have been married for some years and have three children in school. Usually Mr. Walker has seemed cheerful and he and his wife have gotten along pretty well. But lately Mr. Walker has become touchy. He gets irritated very easily and can't sleep nights. He worries about little things and cries a lot, blaming himself for all sorts of things that have gone wrong in the past. Sometimes he keeps Mrs. Walker awake all night long, walking up and down and wringing his hands, talking to her about all the bad things he *thinks* he has done.

Mrs. Walker got him to see a doctor and the doctor told her that he could arrange for Mr. Walker to go to a state mental hospital where a special doctor and nurse would try to make him better in a few months, or she could keep Mr. Walker at home and a special doctor and nurse would come to see him from time to time and try and make him better in a few months. Either way the cost would be about the same. What do you think Mrs. Walker should do? Should she have Mr. Walker sent to the mental hospital or should she keep him at home?

Send to hospital	*49%*
Take care of at home	*46*
Depends	*3*
DK & NA	*2*

What makes you say that?

Change of environment desirable	*14%*
Quality of hospital care better	*34*
Quantity of hospital care better	*12*
Moral obligation to keep at home	*2*
Violence and custody handled better in hospital	*4*
Wife suffers	*1*
Family suffers	*1*
Tender loving care	*1*
Find self in mental hospital awful	*1*

15. Here's the last story. . . . I'd like to know what you think about it. This is about a family living here in Baltimore . . . let's call them the Bakers. Mr. Baker has a good job and he works hard at it. Mrs. Baker stays home and takes care of the house and their two children. Mrs. Baker's mother, a widow of about 70, has been living with them for some years now, ever since her husband died. Lately she has begun to act differently. She forgets things. Sometimes

she even forgets where she is and what year it is. She walks around the house at all hours of the night.

The doctor says that he can arrange for Mrs. Baker's mother to go to a state mental hospital where they have special doctors and nurses to take care of her or he can arrange for her to be taken care of at home by having a special doctor and nurse come to see her from time to time. Either way the cost would be about the same. What should Mr. and Mrs. Baker do? Should they send Mrs. Baker's mother to the mental hospital or should they try to keep her at home?

Send to hospital	*41%*
Take care of at home	*50*
Depends	*5*
DK & NA	*4*

What makes you say that?

Change of environment desirable	*27%*
Quality of hospital care better	*46*
Quantity of hospital care better	*14*
Moral obligation to keep at home	*25*
Violence and custody handled better in hospital	*28*
Family suffers	*43*
Tender loving care	*35*

16. Occupational level

1. Who is the main wage earner in your family?

Respondent (myself)	*46%*
Spouse	*36*
Parent	*6*
Other (SPECIFY)	*11*
DK & NA	*1*

2. What sort of work does (main wage earner) do?

Higher executives, proprietors of large concerns, and major professionals	*4%*
Business managers, proprietors of medium-sized businesses, and lesser professionals	*4*
Administrative personnel, small independent businesses, and minor professionals	*9*
Clerical and sales workers,	

technicians, and owners of little business (value under $6,000)	*12%*
Skilled manual employees	*23*
Machine operators and semiskilled employees	*18*
Unskilled employees	*28*
Housewives	*2*
Students	—
DK & NA	—

17. Education of main wage earner

1. What was the name of the last school attended by [the main wage earner]?
2. What was the last grade [or year] he [she] completed?

Grammar school	*0–4 years*	*10%*
	5–7 years	*18*
	8 years	*15*
High school	*9–11 years*	*22*
	12 years	*17*
College	*1–3 years*	*5*
	4 or more years	*9*
DK & NA		*4*

18. Income

1. Adding together the whole family income, as well as any other money the family here may have received from pensions, unemployment compensation, or other sources, which one of these general groups did the total income of your family fall into during the last twelve months—before taxes, that is?

Under $3,000	*24%*
$3,000–$4,999	*26*
$5,000–$7,499	*29*
More than $7,500	*15*
DK & NA	*6*

19. Home ownership

1. Do you own or rent your home?

Own	*54%*
Rent	*44*

DK & NA	*2%*
Median home value	*$9,071.00*
Median monthly rental	*$63.73*

20. Housing space—crowding

1. How many separate rooms do you have in this [apartment, house] not counting the bathroom?

One	*1%*
Two	*2*
Three	*10*
Four	*13*
Five	*13*
Six	*33*
Seven	*13*
Eight	*9*
Nine	*2*
Ten or more	*4*

21. Birthplace

1. Where were you born?

Foreign country	*5%*
United States	*95*

2. State—Public health regions

Region		
I & II	*Connecticut, Vermont, Massachusetts, Maine, New Hampshire, Rhode Island, Delaware, New York, New Jersey, Pennsylvania*	*7%*
III	*Kentucky, North Carolina, Maryland, Puerto Rico, Virginia, West Virginia, Virgin Islands, District of Columbia*	*77*
IV	*Alabama, Georgia, Florida, Tennessee, South Carolina, Mississippi*	*7*
V	*Illinois, Ohio, Michigan, Indiana, Wisconsin*	*1*
VI	*Iowa, North Dakota, South Dakota, Kansas, Nebraska, Minnesota, Missouri*	*1*
VII	*Arkansas, Texas, Oklahoma, Louisiana, New Mexico*	*1*
VIII	*Colorado, Utah, Idaho, Montana, Wyoming*	—
IX	*Arizona, Washington, California, Alaska, Oregon, Nevada, Hawaii, Guam*	*6*

3. Type of birthplace

City	*61%*
Town	*21*
Farm	*18*

4. Length of time in Baltimore?

Less than one year	*1%*
One to two years	*3*
Three to five years	*4*
More than five years but less than life	*47*
Life	*45*

22. Race

White	*59%*
Negro	*41*
Other	—

APPENDIX B

Baltimore Study and UAW Wave II Tables

'PENDIX TABLE 1. Identification of Three Examples of Mental Illness, by Marital Status (Baltimore, 1960)

,rital atus	Number in Sample	Total Percentage	Number of Examples Identified				Mean Number of Examples Identified	Standard Deviation
			Three	Two	One	None		
,ed	1,162	100.0%	51.0%	34.0%	12.0%	3.0%	2.33	0.80
e	277	100.0	46.0	34.0	16.0	4.0	2.22	0.86
wed	189	100.0	45.0	41.0	9.0	5.0	2.23	0.83
·ced or arated	107	100.0	54.0	33.0	10.0	3.0	2.80	0.78
otal	1,735[a]							

TE: $p < .20$.

Marital status of three cases unknown.

APPENDIX TABLE 2. Identification of Three Examples of Mental Illness, by Length of Time in Baltimore (Baltimore, 1960)

Length of Time in Baltimore	Number in Sample	Total Percentage	Number of Examples Identified				Mean Number of Examples Identified	Standard Deviation
			Three	Two	One	None		
Less than five years	141	100.0%	44.0%	34.0%	17.0%	5.0%	2.17	0.88
More than five years	809	100.0	50.0	35.0	11.0	4.0	2.23	0.81
Since birth	782	100.0	51.0	34.0	12.0	3.0	2.38	0.81
Total	1,732[a]							

NOTE: $p < .50$.

a. Length of time in Baltimore unknown for six residents.

APPENDIX TABLE 3. Identification of Three Examples of Mental Illness, by Occupational Level of Main Wage Earner
(Baltimore, 1960)

Occupational Level	Number in Sample	Total Percentage	Number of Examples Identified				Mean Number of Examples Identified	Standard Deviation
			Three	Two	One	None		
Higher executives, proprietors of large concerns, and major professionals	63	100.0%	73.0%	15.9%	11.1%	—	2.62	0.68
Business managers, proprietors of medium-sized businesses, and lesser professionals	71	100.0	59.2	21.1	15.5	4.2%	2.35	0.98
Administrative personnel, small independent businesses, and minor professionals	155	100.0	47.1	38.0	12.3	2.6	2.30	0.82
Clerical and sales workers, technicians and owners of little businesses	203	100.0	56.3	30.0	10.3	3.4	2.39	0.81
Skilled manual employees	406	100.0	50.0	33.7	13.8	2.5	2.31	0.80
Machine operators and semiskilled employees	305	100.0	46.5	40.7	8.2	4.6	2.29	0.79
Unskilled employees	484	100.0	45.9	37.4	12.4	4.3	2.25	0.71
Housewives	41	100.0	46.3	22.0	24.4	7.3	2.07	1.00
Students	4	100.0	100.0	—	—	—	3.00	0.00
Miscellaneous	4	100.0	100.0	—	—	—	3.00	0.00
Total	1,736[a]							

NOTE: $p < .001$. This table follows the classification in Hollingshead (1957).

a. Occupational level of two main wage earners unknown.

APPENDIX TABLE 4. Social Distance Attitudes Toward Various Referents by Contact: Willingness to Work With (UAW Wave II)

Attitude	Total N	Total Willing	Definitely Willing	Probably Willing	Probably Unwilling	Definitely Unwilling	Total Unwilling
Toward family:							
Normal	23	100%	74%	26%	—	—	—
Male mental patient	57	100	72	28	—	—	—
Female mental patient	53	96	79	17	—	4%	4%
"Someone" patient	58	94	66	28	3%	3	6
Toward relative or friend:							
Normal	26	100	81	19	—	—	—
Male mental patient	45	96	58	38	2	2	4
Female mental patient	52	96	63	33	—	4	4
"Someone" patient	54	98	65	33	2	—	2
Toward acquaintance:							
Normal	12	100	67	33	—	—	—
Male mental patient	40	98	67	31	—	2	2
Female mental patient	32	100	81	19	—	—	—
"Someone" patient	35	100	63	37	—	—	—
Toward all others:							
Normal	12	100	75	25	—	—	—
Male mental patient	59	98	56	42	2	—	2
Female mental patient	50	98	70	26	—	2	2
"Someone" patient	50	96	58	38	2	2	4

NOTE: Tabulations are mutually exclusive. Multiple responses were tabulated in closest relationship. "Don't know" and "no answer" were excluded.

APPENDIX TABLE 5. Social Distance Attitudes Toward Various Referents by Contact: Willingness to Rent Room To (UAW Wave II)

Attitude	Total N	Total Willing	Definitely Willing	Probably Willing	Probably Unwilling	Definitely Unwilling	Total Unwilling
Toward family:							
Normal	23	96%	61%	35%	—	4%	4%
Male mental patient	56	86	36	50	13%	2	15
Female mental patient	53	90	51	40	6	4	10
"Someone" patient	58	81	19	62	10	9	19
Toward relative or friend:							
Normal	27	97	56	41	—	3	3
Male mental patient	45	75	33	42	16	9	25
Female mental patient	51	88	37	41	6	16	22
"Someone" patient	53	83	26	57	6	11	17
Toward acquaintance:							
Normal	12	83	50	33	—	17	17
Male mental patient	41	83	44	39	12	5	17
Female mental patient	32	78	53	25	9	13	22
"Someone" patient	34	70	23	47	24	6	30
Toward all others:							
Normal	12	83	50	33	17	—	17
Male mental patient	59	85	16	69	10	5	15
Female mental patient	50	84	40	44	6	10	16
"Someone" patient	42	81	29	52	12	7	19

NOTE: Tabulations are mutually exclusive. Multiple responses were tabulated in closest relationship. "Don't know" and "no answer" were excluded.

APPENDIX TABLE 6. Social Distance Attitudes Toward Various Referents by Contact: Willingness to Have Child Marry
(UAW Wave II)

Attitude	Total N	Total Willing	Definitely Willing	Probably Willing	Probably Unwilling	Definitely Unwilling	Total Unwilling
Toward family:							
Normal	22	100%	64%	36%	—	—	—
Male mental patient	55	80	22	58	16%	4%	20%
Female mental patient	59	71	29	42	22	7	29
"Someone" patient	58	59	10	48	31	10	41
Toward relative or friend:							
Normal	26	93	70	27	3	—	3
Male mental patient	44	71	23	48	20	9	29
Female mental patient	51	70	31	39	16	14	30
"Someone" patient	53	63	9	57	23	11	34
Toward acquaintance:							
Normal	12	99	45	54	9	—	9
Male mental patient	41	81	15	66	12	7	19
Female mental patient	32	82	44	38	12	6	18
"Someone" patient	34	71	9	62	21	8	29
Toward all others:							
Normal	12	100	42	58	—	—	—
Male mental patient	59	78	14	64	17	5	22
Female mental patient	50	80	30	50	12	8	20
"Someone" patient	41	63	19	44	17	20	37

NOTE: Tabulations are mutually exclusive. Multiple responses were tabulated in closest relationship. "Don't know" and "no answer" were excluded.

APPENDIX TABLE 7. Social Distance Attitudes Toward Various Referents by Education of Respondent: Willingness to Work With
(UAW Wave II)

Attitude	Total N	Total Willing	Definitely Willing	Probably Willing	Probably Unwilling	Definitely Unwilling	Total Unwilling
Of grade 8 and under toward:							
Normal	18	100%	83%	17%	—	—	—
Male mental patient	57	98	63	35	—	2%	2%
Female mental patient	56	95	77	18	—	5	5
"Someone" patient	55	94	60	34	2%	4	6
Of grades 9 to 11 toward:							
Normal	25	100	76	24	—	—	—
Male mental patient	79	98	70	28	2	—	2
Female mental patient	67	100	76	24	—	—	—
"Someone" patient	58	98	65	33	—	2	2
Of grade 12 and over toward:							
Normal	30	100	70	30	—	—	—
Male mental patient	64	98	56	42	—	2	2
Female mental patient	64	95	65	30	—	5	5
"Someone" patient	77	96	60	36	4	—	4

APPENDIX TABLE 8. Social Distance Attitudes Toward Various Referents by Education of Respondent: Willingness to Rent Room To (UAW Wave II)

Attitude	Total N	Total Willing	Definitely Willing	Probably Willing	Probably Unwilling	Definitely Unwilling	Total Unwilling
Of grade 8 and under toward:							
Normal	18	88%	77%	11%	6%	6%	12%
Male mental patient	60	83	33	50	10	7	17
Female mental patient	56	78	43	34	7	16	23
"Someone" patient	51	78	25	53	10	12	22
Of grades 9 to 11 toward:							
Normal	25	92	48	44	—	8	8
Male mental patient	77	85	30	55	10	5	15
Female mental patient	66	86	50	36	9	5	14
"Someone" patient	58	90	29	61	3	7	10
Of grade 12 and over toward:							
Normal	31	94	49	45	3	3	6
Male mental patient	54	76	17	59	20	4	24
Female mental patient	64	86	41	45	3	11	14
"Someone" patient	76	75	20	55	20	5	25

APPENDIX TABLE 9. Social Distance Attitudes Toward Various Referents by Education of Respondent: Willingness to Have Child Marry
(UAW Wave II)

Attitude	Total N	Total Willing	Definitely Willing	Probably Willing	Probably Unwilling	Definitely Unwilling	Total Unwilling
Of grade 8 and under toward:							
Normal	18	94%	77%	17%	6%	—	6%
Male mental patient	59	73	20	53	22	5%	27
Female mental patient	56	66	29	37	20	14	34
"Someone" patient	51	61	18	43	18	21	39
Of grades 9 to 11 toward:							
Normal	24	96	54	42	—	4	4
Male mental patient	77	80	18	62	14	6	20
Female mental patient	66	86	35	51	12	2	14
"Someone" patient	58	69	16	53	22	9	31
Of grade 12 and over toward:							
Normal	30	100	50	50	—	—	—
Male mental patient	63	80	16	64	14	6	20
Female mental patient	64	78	36	42	9	13	22
"Someone" patient	58	69	16	53	22	9	31

APPENDIX TABLE 10. Social Distance Attitudes Toward Various Referents by Sex of Respondent: Willingness to Work With
(UAW Wave II)

Attitude	Total N	Total Willing	Definitely Willing	Probably Willing	Probably Unwilling	Definitely Unwilling	Total Unwilling
Of males toward:							
Normal	42	100%	76%	24%	—	—	—
Male mental patient	98	97	65	32	2%	1%	3%
Female mental patient	103	96	66	30	—	4	4
"Someone" patient	102	96	60	36	1	3	4
Of females toward:							
Normal	31	100	74	26	—	—	—
Male mental patient	104	99	61	38	—	1	1
Female mental patient	84	98	81	17	—	2	2
"Someone" patient	87	97	64	33	3	—	3

APPENDIX TABLE 11. Social Distance Attitudes Toward Various Referents by Sex of Respondent: Willingness to Rent Room To
(UAW Wave II)

Attitude	Total N	Total Willing	Definitely Willing	Probably Willing	Probably Unwilling	Definitely Unwilling	Total Unwilling
Of males toward:							
Normal	42	93%	55%	38%	2%	5%	7%
Male mental patient	96	82	32	50	12	6	18
Female mental patient	102	79	48	31	7	14	21
"Someone" patient	100	78	25	53	11	11	22
Of females toward:							
Normal	32	91	57	34	3	6	9
Male mental patient	105	83	30	53	13	4	17
Female mental patient	84	88	40	48	6	6	12
"Someone" patient	87	81	23	58	13	6	19

APPENDIX TABLE 12. Social Distance Attitudes Toward Various Referents by Sex of Respondent: Willingness to Have Child Marry
(UAW Wave II)

Attitude	Total N	Total Willing	Definitely Willing	Probably Willing	Probably Unwilling	Definitely Unwilling	Total Unwilling
Of males toward:							
Normal	40	98%	55%	43%	—	2%	2%
Male mental patient	96	77	22	55	17%	6	23
Female mental patient	103	79	41	38	11	10	21
"Someone" patient	101	65	11	54	18	17	35
Of females toward:							
Normal	32	97	63	34	3	—	3
Male mental patient	103	78	15	63	16	6	22
Female mental patient	83	76	24	52	16	8	24
"Someone" patient	85	62	13	49	31	7	38

APPENDIX TABLE 13. Social Distance Attitudes Toward Various Referents by Income of Respondent: Willingness to Work With (UAW Wave II)

Attitude	Total N	Total Willing	Definitely Willing	Probably Willing	Probably Unwilling	Definitely Unwilling	Total Unwilling
Of less than $7,500 toward:							
Normal	24	100%	75%	25%	—	—	—
Male mental patient	58	96	56	40	2%	2%	4%
Female mental patient	66	98	77	21	—	2	2
"Someone" patient	55	96	58	38	—	4	4
Of from $7,500 to $10,000 toward:							
Normal	31	100	61	39	—	—	—
Male mental patient	95	100	66	34	—	—	—
Female mental patient	80	95	66	29	—	5	5
"Someone" patient	83	97	64	33	2	1	3
Of over $10,000 toward:							
Normal	18	100	100	—	—	—	—
Male mental patient	49	96	63	33	2	2	4
Female mental patient	41	98	78	20	—	2	2
"Someone" patient	51	96	61	35	4	—	4

APPENDIX TABLE 14. Social Distance Attitudes Toward Various Referents by Income of Respondent: Willingness to Rent Room To-
(UAW Wave II)

Attitude	Total N	Total Willing	Definitely Willing	Probably Willing	Probably Unwilling	Definitely Unwilling	Total Unwilling
Of less than $7,500 toward:							
Normal	24	92%	54%	38%	—	8%	8%
Male mental patient	57	79	30	49	16%	5	21
Female mental patient	60	81	51	30	7	12	19
"Someone" patient	55	78	22	56	13	9	22
Of from $7,500 to $10,000 toward:							
Normal	32	91	41	50	6	3	9
Male mental patient	94	83	29	54	15	2	17
Female mental patient	80	86	41	45	4	10	14
"Someone" patient	82	83	26	57	7	10	17
Of over $10,000 toward:							
Normal	18	94	83	11	—	6	6
Male mental patient	49	86	37	49	4	10	14
Female mental patient	40	82	47	35	10	8	18
"Someone" patient	50	76	24	52	18	6	24

APPENDIX TABLE 15. Social Distance Attitudes Toward Various Referents by Income of Respondent: Willingness to Have Child Marry (UAW Wave II)

Attitude	Total N	Total Willing	Definitely Willing	Probably Willing	Probably Unwilling	Definitely Unwilling	Total Unwilling
Of less than $7,500 toward:							
Normal	22	95%	59%	36%	5%	—	5%
Male mental patient	56	74	21	53	21	5%	26
Female mental patient	65	71	29	42	18	11	29
"Someone" patient	53	55	15	40	30	15	45
Of from $7,500 to $10,000 toward:							
Normal	32	97	47	50	—	3	3
Male mental patient	95	80	16	64	16	4	20
Female mental patient	80	83	35	48	11	6	17
"Someone" patient	82	68	13	55	21	11	32
Of over $10,000 toward:							
Normal	18	100	78	22	—	—	—
Male mental patient	47	78	19	59	11	11	22
Female mental patient	41	78	37	41	10	12	22
"Someone" patient	51	67	6	61	21	12	33

APPENDIX TABLE 16. Social Distance Attitudes Toward Various Referents by Age of Respondent: Willingness to Work With
(UAW Wave II)

Attitude	Total N	Total Willing	Definitely Willing	Probably Willing	Probably Unwilling	Definitely Unwilling	Total Unwilling
Of less than 30 years toward:							
Normal	18	100%	56%	44%	—	—	—
Male mental patient	40	97	62	35	—	3%	3%
Female mental patient	46	98	68	30	—	2	2
"Someone" patient	46	94	57	37	4%	2	6
Of from 31 to 40 years toward:							
Normal	35	100	89	11	—	—	—
Male mental patient	109	97	62	35	2	1	3
Female mental patient	80	97	72	25	—	3	3
"Someone" patient	85	98	59	39	1	1	2
Of from 41 to 50 years toward:							
Normal	16	100	69	31	—	—	—
Male mental patient	43	100	65	35	—	—	—
Female mental patient	44	95	70	25	—	5	5
"Someone" patient	41	100	76	24	—	—	—
Of over 50 years toward:							
Normal	4	100	75	25	—	—	—
Male mental patient	10	100	60	40	—	—	—
Female mental patient	17	94	94	—	—	6	6
"Someone" patient	17	88	53	35	6	6	12

APPENDIX TABLE 17. Social Distance Attitudes Toward Various Referents by Age of Respondent: Willingness to Rent Room To (UAW Wave II)

Attitude	Total N	Total Willing	Definitely Willing	Probably Willing	Probably Unwilling	Definitely Unwilling	Total Unwilling
Of less than 30 years toward:							
Normal	19	90%	32%	58%	5%	5%	10%
Male mental patient	40	82	30	52	15	3	18
Female mental patient	46	96	41	55	2	2	4
"Someone" patient	45	76	20	56	11	13	24
Of from 31 to 40 years toward:							
Normal	35	94	66	28	3	3	6
Male mental patient	108	88	31	57	8	4	12
Female mental patient	79	82	47	35	8	10	18
"Someone" patient	84	77	20	57	15	8	23
Of from 41 to 50 years toward:							
Normal	16	87	56	31	—	13	13
Male mental patient	42	71	31	40	19	10	29
Female mental patient	44	75	41	34	9	16	25
"Someone" patient	41	96	39	57	2	2	4
Of over 50 years toward:							
Normal	4	100	75	25	—	—	—
Male mental patient	11	73	27	46	18	9	27
Female mental patient	17	76	53	23	6	18	24
"Someone" patient	17	70	18	52	18	12	30

APPENDIX TABLE 18. Social Distance Attitudes Toward Various Referents by Age of Respondent: Willingness to Have Child Marry
(UAW Wave II)

Attitude	Total N	Total Willing	Definitely Willing	Probably Willing	Probably Unwilling	Definitely Unwilling	Total Unwilling
Of less than 30 years toward:							
Normal	18	100%	28%	72%	—	—	—
Male mental patient	40	80	17	63	17%	3%	20%
Female mental patient	46	91	37	54	7	2	9
"Someone" patient	46	71	11	60	20	9	29
Of from 31 to 40 years toward:							
Normal	34	100	71	29	—	—	—
Male mental patient	107	84	21	63	12	4	16
Female mental patient	79	78	32	46	16	6	22
"Someone" patient	84	60	12	48	27	13	40
Of from 41 to 50 years toward:							
Normal	16	88	63	25	6	6	12
Male mental patient	42	67	14	53	19	14	33
Female mental patient	44	68	34	34	16	16	32
"Someone" patient	40	75	15	60	15	10	25
Of over 50 years toward:							
Normal	4	100	75	25	—	—	—
Male mental patient	10	40	10	30	50	10	60
Female mental patient	17	64	29	35	12	24	36
"Someone" patient	17	35	6	29	41	24	65

APPENDIX C

Correlations of Baltimore Study

APPENDIX TABLE 19. All Correlations Among Twenty-One Selected

Question/Statement	2	3	4	7-1	7-2	7-3	7-4	7-5	12-1
Identification questions									
2. Simple schizophrenic	1.00	0.24	0.18	0.02	0.01	0.03	0.01	0.10	0.02
3. Alcoholic		1.00	0.15	0.04	0.04	0.17	0.06	0.07	0.04
4. Paranoid			1.00	0.03	0.07	0.03	0.07	0.01	0.01
Attitude statements									
7-1. Not marry mentally ill				1.00	0.29	0.35	0.19	0.16	0.12
7-2. Could love mentally ill					1.00	0.39	0.25	0.10	0.18
7-3. Room with mentally ill						1.00	0.33	0.28	0.15
7-4. Work with mentally ill							1.00	0.21	0.16
7-5. Might work in mental hospital								1.00	0.03
12-1. Hospitalize all mentally ill									1.00
12-2. Most mentally ill are dangerous									
12-3. Guard mentally ill in institution									
12-4. Lock up mentally ill patients									
12-5. Many kinds of mentally ill									
12-6. All mentally ill act alike									
12-7. Some mental patients need home care									
12-8. Sometimes home care for mental patients									
12-9. If family member mentally ill, needs home care									
12-10. Mental patients are not criminal									
Home-care questions									
13. Depressed									
14. Involutional depression									
15. Senile									

Note: See Appendix A for text of questions.

Responses for 1,738 Respondents (Baltimore, 1960)

12-2	12-3	12-4	12-5	12-6	12-7	12-8	12-9	12-10	13	14	15	
0.04	0.01	0.06	0.04	0.01	0.02	0.04	0.03	0.00	0.03	0.03	0.03	2.
0.05	0.04	0.03	0.04	0.04	0.06	0.05	0.06	0.06	0.00	0.01	0.01	3.
0.01	0.03	0.04	0.08	0.00	0.01	0.01	0.05	0.04	0.02	0.04	0.02	4.
0.21	0.23	0.22	0.02	0.10	0.01	0.09	0.06	0.10	0.04	0.05	0.03	7-1.
0.19	0.17	0.18	0.06	0.06	0.07	0.04	0.04	0.11	0.11	0.00	0.02	7-2.
0.21	0.26	0.21	0.01	0.03	0.02	0.07	0.03	0.10	0.05	0.03	0.03	7-3.
0.23	0.20	0.23	0.04	0.16	0.06	0.11	0.11	0.02	0.05	0.04	0.06	7-4.
0.04	0.07	0.04	0.02	0.00	0.02	0.04	0.05	0.03	0.03	0.06	0.02	7-5.
0.41	0.39	0.34	0.04	0.22	0.24	0.28	0.19	0.12	0.18	0.13	0.17	12-1.
1.00	0.36	0.36	0.06	0.22	0.11	0.15	0.12	0.08	0.13	0.06	0.10	12-2.
	1.00	0.45	0.02	0.14	0.04	0.15	0.11	0.07	0.11	0.04	0.10	12-3.
		1.00	0.02	0.24	0.09	0.11	0.09	0.04	0.21	0.10	0.13	12-4.
			1.00	0.18	0.08	0.08	0.10	0.06	0.02	0.04	0.04	12-5.
				1.00	0.10	0.06	0.04	0.01	0.05	0.05	0.04	12-6.
					1.00	0.41	0.37	0.13	0.17	0.10	0.03	12-7.
						1.00	0.41	0.09	0.19	0.08	0.06	12-8.
							1.00	0.08	0.16	0.08	0.00	12-9.
								1.00	0.00	0.02	0.01	12-10.
									1.00	0.32	0.15	13.
										1.00	0.15	14.
											1.00	15.

APPENDIX TABLE 20. Social Position and Race (Baltimore, 1960)

Social Position	White	Nonwhite
I and II	2.6%	0.6%
III	19.4	8.7
IV	42.7	22.7
V	35.3	68.0

NOTE: This table follows the classification in Hollingshead (1957). This classification is obtained by assigning a weight to the occupation and to the years of education of the main wage earner. The inference was made that the Index of Social Position scores should cut at the point of most heterogeneity in the scale's score pattern. Four classes emerged from the analysis. Classes I and II were combined because of the small numbers that were found in class I. The assumed social classes ranged from the highest (classes I and II) to the lowest (class V). For a further discussion of this, see Hollingshead and Redlich (1958, appendix 3, "Social Stratification and Mass Communication").

APPENDIX TABLE 21. Sex, Age, and Family Size of UAW Workers by Postal Zone of Residence

		All Other Zones				
Characteristic	Sample Zones	Total or Average	1	2	3	4
Population[a]						
Percentage	60%	40%	13%	11%	9%	7%
Number	2,892	1,935	623	528	435	349
Sex						
Male	52%	52%	52%	51%	53%	53%
Female	48%	48%	48%	48%	47%	47%
Average age (all family members)	23.6	23.4	23.7	23.5	23.2	23.1
Average age (adults 21 to 60)	40.2	40.2	40.2	40.0	40.1	40.3
Average family size	3.7	3.6	3.6	3.7	3.6	3.4

a. The total population = 4,827.

APPENDIX TABLE 22. Marital Status of Census-Tract Population, UAW Sample, and Neighbors

	Census Tracts[a] (N = 106,391)	UAW Sample (N = 888)	Neighbors (N = 63)
Single	19%	7%	5%
Married	70	86	78
Widowed	3	3	13
Separated or divorced	8	4	5
Total	100%	100%	100%

a. U.S. Bureau of the Census 1960.

APPENDIX TABLE 23. Annual Family Income of Census-Tract Population, UAW Sample, and Neighbors

	Census Tracts (N = 5,837)[a]	UAW Sample (N = 888)	Neighbors (N = 63)
Under $3,000	10%	2%	1%
$3,000 to $4,999	21	2	3
$5,000 to $7,499	38	18	27
$7,500 to $10,000	19	41	44
Over $10,000	12	24	18
No answer	—	13	7
Total	100%	100%	100%
Average income	$6,377	$8,708	$7,662

a. Based on 20 percent sample in U.S. Bureau of the Census 1960.

APPENDIX TABLE 24. Responses of UAW Respondents and Their Neighbors to Five Authoritarian Statements

Statement	UAW (N = 888)	Neighbors (N = 63)
The most important thing to teach children is absolute obedience to parents.		
Agree	70%	70%
Disagree	21	25
Don't know, no answer	9	5
Good leaders should be strict to gain respect.		
Agree	58	62
Disagree	33	30
Don't know, no answer	9	8
There are two kinds of people in the world, the weak and the strong.		
Agree	57	49
Disagree	33	43
Don't know, no answer	10	8
Prison is too good for sex criminals. They should be publicly whipped or worse.		
Agree	26	49
Disagree	59	43
Don't know, no answer	15	8
No decent man can respect a woman who has premarital sex relations.		
Agree	20	27
Disagree	67	62
Don't know, no answer	13	11

NOTE: Statements are from Adorno et al. 1950.

APPENDIX TABLE 25. Voting Behavior of UAW Respondents and Their Neighbors

	UAW (N = 888)	Neighbors (N = 63)
Voted for president in 1964:		
Yes	50%	54%
No	41%	44%
No answer	9%	2%
Voted for president in 1968:		
Yes	54%	54%
No	38%	43%
No answer	8%	3%
Total N who voted (1968)	478	34
Candidate voted for (1968):		
Humphrey	47%	45%
Nixon	26%	31%
Wallace	19%	14%
No answer	8%	10%

APPENDIX D

Methods of Baltimore and UAW Studies

In chapters 1 and 2 we surveyed the literature on the public's attitudes toward the mentally ill and outlined the development of a "theory of rejection" of the mentally ill in the works of Star, Clausen, and the Cummings. Five corollaries of the "theory of rejection" were brought out as hypotheses. Following the discussion of questionnaire designs in a description of the samples and their field execution, we will describe the methods by which the present studies tested these corollaries.

The questionnaires under scrutiny are the 1960 general survey of the Baltimore population (hereafter referred to as the Baltimore study) and the 1968 and 1970 studies of members of the United Automobile Workers of America in the Baltimore area (hereafter jointly referred to as the UAW study or individually as Wave I or Wave II of same). The questions are discussed together. The samples and study designs are different and will be dealt with separately.

Questionnaire Design[1]

The hypothesis that the public will avoid seeing evidence of mental illness is primarily derived from the findings of Star (1955b) and the Cummings (1957). Both of these studies

1. The questionnaire of the Baltimore study can be found in Appendix A.

used a series of six vignettes describing typical cases of various mental illnesses as a test of the respondent's ability to identify mental illness. Developed by Star and Clausen in consultation with a group of psychiatrists, these case descriptions have become virtually a standard test of this ability. Three of the vignettes were used without alteration in the Baltimore study. The full texts are given in chapter 3.

The ability to identify mental illness in the three vignettes was measured by response to the question: "Would you say this [man/woman, name of subject] has some kind of mental illness—a sickness of the mind—or not?" The wording used by Star was "Would you say that this [man/woman, name of subject] has some kind of mental illness or not?"

The testing of the hypothesis that the public will deny contact with the mentally ill is completely straightforward. Since it is what respondents say rather than what they do that is at issue, responses provide a direct test of the hypothesis. In the Baltimore study respondents were asked: "Have you ever known anyone who was in a hospital for mental illness?" Affirmative answers were then probed. For purposes of this report the key probe was: "Was this a relative, close friend, or someone you didn't know very well?"

In the UAW study a series of questions was asked about this issue. First of all, the experience of the respondent, his spouse, or his dependent children living in the same household was traced in detail. This series of questions covered hospitalization, consulting a psychiatrist, consulting a nonpsychiatric physician about any nervous or mental problem, or discussing such a problem with a psychologist, marriage counselor, or priest or minister. Each of the contacts was then probed in considerable detail.

Irrespective of their answers to the first series of questions, respondents were also asked whether they had ever known anyone who had been hospitalized for a mental illness. They were also asked if they had ever known anyone who had consulted a psychiatrist. In addition, they were asked if they had ever known anyone who was not receiving treatment who they thought was mentally ill. Each affirmative answer to these questions was probed by asking: "*Who* was that, a relative, close friend, or just someone you know?" The answers to all of these questions were completely coded so that various types of nonduplicating counts as well as overall totals could be established.

Willingness to admit contact with the mentally ill was also explored by including in the sample all the active clinic patients. Patients were not aware of the reason for their inclusion in the survey, nor were interviewers aware that they were interviewing clinic patients. These patients were asked the same questions as described above.

The third hypothesis held is that the public has a stereotyped view of the mentally ill as dangerous and fear-provoking. This is a fairly general idea and was approached in a number of ways in the Baltimore study. First a series of seven statements was selected from previous studies. After pretesting, these statements were presented in randomly differing order to each respondent, who was asked to agree or disagree with each one. The amount of stereotypy was explored by statements about whether there were many different types of mental illness and whether all people with the same mental illness acted the same way.

Five statements examined the respondent's fear of the mentally ill by asking for a response to statements that everyone with a mental illness should be placed in a mental hospital, that almost all persons who have a mental illness are dangerous, and that mental hospitals should use locked doors, high fences, and guards. Another statement inquired whether a former mental hospital patient was more likely to commit crimes than other people. Whatever else they might reflect, the responses to such statements would seem certain to detect any general stereotyped feeling that the mentally ill were dangerous or to be feared and thus isolated as the Cummings have argued (1957).

Of course, a desire to isolate the mentally ill might conceivably manifest itself as other than a direct fear of them. However indirect the fear or desire to isolate might be, it could not but affect the public's attitudes toward home care of the mentally ill vis-à-vis hospitalization and the reasons for offered attitudes. These were assessed by questions based on case descriptions of a severely depressed young girl, an involutional depressed male breadwinner, and an elderly senile woman (texts in Appendix A). After each of these vignettes had been read and the respondents had been told that the doctor had said that both the cost and prognosis of home care and hospitalization were the same, they were asked to recommend a treatment plan for the case. An open-ended probe of the reasons for the answers was also included. In addition, three agree-or-disagree statements about the home care of the mentally ill were included in another part of the questionnaire.

As indicated in the discussion of the sick role in chapter 2, it is not always a simple matter to determine what the sick role is. In the present studies questions with two different approaches were used to test the hypothesis that the public denies the mentally ill the sick role. The more indirect questions stemmed from the assumption that advising someone to see a doctor and assigning him the sick role are closely related if not identical. Following the presentation of the Star vignettes in the Baltimore survey, the respondents were asked if they thought the described person should see a doctor. The UAW respondents on the other hand were asked whether they thought people who are mentally ill required a doctor's care just as much as people who have a physical illness.

Both studies also inquired into the respondent's beliefs about the curability of the mentally ill as further indirect evidence related to the granting of the sick role to the mentally ill. Responses to these latter statements were also used to measure the respondent's pessimism about mental illness. This is related directly to the hypothesis of the persistent stigmatization of the mentally ill.

The investigation of the hypothesis that the public rejects social intimacy with the mentally ill involves the concept of social distance. For the purposes of this appendix it is sufficient to consider that social distance may be measured in a somewhat scalar fashion of differential acceptance in accordance with the intimacy of the projected relationship. The idea is more fully developed in chapters 6 and 8. The material used in both studies consisted of some identification of a referent whose social distance from the respondent was to be measured and a series of hypothetical social situations or relationships in whose context the respondent was to evaluate the referent's acceptability. As with any relative measurement, it is important to establish some sort of base line so that the rejection experienced by a particular group may be put into its proper perspective.

In the Baltimore study the referent used was "someone who had been mentally ill" in four of its five relationships ranging from "working with" to "having one of your children marry," and "someone who had been in a mental hospital" for the statement about "rooming with." The stronger wording of the latter statement is of interest in revealing the bias of the 1960 investigators, who began the study with an uncritical assumption of the truth of the "theory of rejection" (Crocetti and Lemkau 1963). The questionnaire was developed inductively through extensive pretesting. The pretest results showed what seemed to be an unusually high acceptance of "someone who had been mentally ill" in the fairly close relationship of "rooming with." This was attributed to the nonrepresentative nature of the pretest sample. However, as an additional precaution the referent was made more explicit. It was with surprise, therefore, at the conclusion of the study, that the results on this statement were found to be the same as that obtained with the pretest wording—"someone who had been mentally ill." In each case the respondent simply replied to the statement that he would or would not be willing to accept the described person in such a relationship.

The work of Phillips (1963) had emphasized the need for a firmer idea of the acceptance of a "normal" person. Some of the findings of Elinson, Padilla, and Perkins (1967) suggested that a dichotomous format might be inadequate for measuring social-distance response. The validity of this doubt is discussed in chapter 8. These considerations and other doubts about the effects of changes in the characteristics of the referent explain the design of the social-distance questions used in the second wave of the UAW survey.

In the first wave of the UAW study, three social-distance questions were used. Their referent was "someone who had been mentally ill" and they concerned the relationships of "working with," "rooming with," and "falling in love with." In contrast to the statements of the Baltimore study, the respondents were given a fourfold choice of answers.

The same respondents were resurveyed eighteen months later. In the resurvey four different referents were used in four random subsamples of the panel. The first of these was a description of a "normal" person. This description was identical with the one used by Phillips (1963). It was intended to provide a base line. The second was exactly the same description except for the addition of the sentence: "He is generally healthy enough although he was once in a hospital for mental illness."

Some evidence from the 1960 study and from Phillips (1963) suggested that there might be some difference in response according to the sex of the referent. Accordingly the third version simply changed the sex of the referent from male to female ex-patient. The fourth referent was exactly the same as that used in the first wave of the UAW study.

In the resurvey five points of social distance were used for all referents. These ranged from "neighbor" to "having one of your children marry." One of the points "working with" was identically the same as in the first wave of the survey. Another was changed only slightly from "rooming with" to "renting a room in your home to." The point of minimal social distance in the first wave of surveying was "falling in love with"; in the resurvey the minimal point was "having one of your children marry."

The assumption is that differences in response, beyond those attributable to sampling, are due to the different versions of the questions. The addition of the phrase "once a patient in a mental hospital" to an identically worded description of the "normal" person is assumed to be responsible for any difference in response of the population. Differences between male and female ex-patients and the "someone" ex-patient are similarly interpreted in chapter 8.

The proper positioning of the additional sentence stating that the referent was a former mental patient was a matter of some concern. It could be neither so prominent as to "cue" the respondent nor so "buried" as to be forgotten in the respondent's consideration of his answer. Accordingly, all versions of all social-distance questions were pretested on working-class populations not included in the sample. The pretest interviewers were specially trained to probe each answer nondirectively to the point where the frame of reference from which the respondent was answering could be reasonably inferred. For example, if the response was "definitely willing" to renting a room to a former mental patient, the interviewer would ask: "Why do you say that?" If the respondent answered, "Well, whatever was wrong with him he seems to be over it now," it would be assumed that in his answer he had not lost sight of the fact that the referent was a former mental patient and that consequently the question was being responded to in a suitable manner. Contingencies, such as not having a room to rent or having no children, were met by the probe, "Well, supposing. . . ." The final decision as to the positioning of the sentence containing the information that the referent was a former mental patient was not arrived at until twenty consecutive pretest interviews had shown that the questions were "working" properly.

Sample and Fieldwork Techniques of the Baltimore Study

The design of the study was relatively simple. A randomly selected sample of the population of Baltimore, Maryland, was interviewed by specially trained professional interviewers, with the interviewer reading a preformulated questionnaire in a more or less conversational and relaxed home setting. Seven hundred and forty-seven individuals were interviewed. Responses were obtained for 90.2 percent of all selected respondents. Two experienced statisticians were consulted in the selection of the population sample.

The sample was selected by listing all the blocks in Baltimore, classifying them according to the number of people living in the block, and then within each classification selecting a given number of blocks by random means. All of the dwelling units on each block selected were then listed by enumerators who inspected the block. Again by random means, a number of dwelling units were selected from each block. Interviewers were then assigned these addresses. The particular individuals living at the address were ascertained by personal interview and the specific respondent was selected by random means from the list of those over eighteen years of age in the dwelling unit. Individuals so selected were the people who answered the questionnaire.

For purposes of direct tabulations the questionnaires were weighted by the number of adults living in the dwelling unit. This resulted in a total N of 1,737. However, comparisons used in computation are from the unweighted sample. Throughout the development of the questionnaire, there was frequent consultation with psychiatrists working in Baltimore, and with experts with many years of experience in the construction of questionnaires and in studying popular opinion.

Interviewing for the study was done by a commercial interviewing service on a contract basis. The interviewers averaged 5.4 years of experience in this type of work. As an initial step in their training, all interviewers completed the questionnaire using each other as respondents. (Their answers were later compared to the answers of the individuals they interviewed, and no significant bias, either for or against their own opinions, was found.) The interviewers were given an intensive two-day training session on the use of the protocol, which was conducted by an experienced field supervisor. Each then conducted trial interviews with persons not in the sample, and these interviews were evaluated to determine the interviewer's ability to use the protocol as instructed. Approximately 20 percent of all interviews in the study group were verified; that is, respondents were reinterviewed by telephone or personal visit. No instance of interviewer "cheating" was found.

The sample was poorly educated with the median number of years of education being 9.7. Forty percent of the sample were black, the majority of whom had migrated to Baltimore from farther south. The median family income for the entire sample was $4,730. The median age was in the early forties. Approximately 55 percent of the respondents owned their homes, and the median value of the homes was $9,901. The median rental for those who rented was about $64 per month. In other words, the sample population was neither a highly educated nor an especially well-to-do group.

Forty-one percent of the respondents were males; 59 percent were females. Sixty-seven percent were married; 17 percent were widowed, divorced, or separated; and the remainder were single. In 30 percent of the households there were children under five years of age. Eighty-seven percent of the households presented a fairly typical family constellation, that is, the husband and wife and the children were present. Seven percent of the households consisted only of mother and children, and in the remaining 6 percent it was not possible to determine the family constellation from the enumeration report. Forty-one percent of the respondents were actually the heads of the household. In 34 percent of the families there was only one generation present. In 50 percent of the families two generations were present, and in 14 percent, three or more generations shared the same dwelling unit.

Fifty-nine percent of the respondents were white; 41 percent were black. This compares with a 1960 Baltimore census distribution of 61 percent white and 39 percent black. The median family income of the white members of the sample was $5,650; for the black members it was $4,000.

The white members of the sample had a median of 9.3 years of education and the black members, 8.5 years. Twenty-three percent of the main wage earners in the sample had some high school education. Forty-two percent had less than a high school education. Seventeen percent had completed high school. Fourteen percent had some college. Almost one-half of the respondents had only an elementary school education or less.

The study design limited possible respondents to those eighteen years of age and over. The sample, on the whole, was significantly younger than the overall population of Baltimore. However, the percentage in each broad age category is approximately the same for both the city population and the sample. The difference in median age is due to the fact that the sample underrepresented those in the fifty to fifty-nine age group.

Hollingshead's "Two-Factor Index of Social Position" (1957) was used to group the sample into the five basic social classes that Hollingshead himself had used. The percentage of the sample falling in each social class, by race, is shown in appendix table 20. The number of individuals in social classes I and II were so few that they were combined. As can be seen from the table, almost half of the respondents fall in class V. Over half of the nonwhite respondents are in class V. The distribution of the white respondents is more typical of the distribution one would expect for the country or a metropolitan area as a whole. This study, however, was confined within the political boundaries of Baltimore itself, which is essentially the core city of the Baltimore metropolitan area. Thus, one would expect an overrepresentation of Hollingshead's class V group, which in core cities is largely black.

Sample and Fieldwork Techniques of the UAW Study

The purpose of the survey was to evaluate the impact on a blue-collar population of prepaid comprehensive psychiatric care. The insured were members of the United Automobile Workers. This population is representative of neither the general population of the Baltimore region nor the working-class population of the area. The UAW members were chosen for study because of a unique opportunity to survey a worker population while providing all mental health services for that population.

The insured group consisted of 4,827 workers and their families. All but forty-two of these families lived in seven of forty postal zones of the Baltimore metropolitan region. The areas of residence stretched in a roughly semicircular shape around the two plants where the UAW members were employed. More than three-quarters of the area is outside the city limits and within Baltimore County; this was an important factor in sample decision. In Baltimore proper most blocks are roughly rectangular, streets and avenues are in an east-west or north-south designation, and a system of parallel numbering of addresses is used. Within the city limits, it is possible to select a probability cluster based simply on address. The relative distance between two addresses can be easily established.

The same is not true in Baltimore County. In the county there are many short roads and many winding roads; north-south or east-west designation is rare; and numerical designation of addresses is not parallel. In the present study the only method of obtaining a cluster sample of such an area from a list of addresses is through a spot map of all addresses. A trial of this method for the UAW population quickly indicated that the economy of fieldwork that might be achieved by clustering would be more than absorbed in the clerical effort of locating the majority of addresses on a map.

An examination of the postal zones of residence showed that even within the seven postal zones that included virtually the entire population, the workers were not evenly distributed. About 60 percent, or almost three thousand of the workers, lived in three of the seven zones most accessible to their place of work. These three zones were adjacent to each other. It was obvious that if sampling could be confined to these three zones, economy of clustering would be achieved. Such a method of selection would not yield a probability sample of the entire universe of insured. However, the real problem was whether such a restriction would compromise the integrity of the sample in a meaningful way.

The population to be sampled was listed on IBM printouts provided by Blue Cross, the insurance carrier. From these printouts it was possible to determine, age, marital status, family size, and postal zone of residence. The population being studied was already homogeneous in occupation, income, and place of work. It was decided to compare the workers residing in these three zones with those residing in other postal zones in terms of age, marital status, and family size. If the comparison showed no significant differences, then it would be reasonable to select a random sample of the workers residing in the three postal zones with the heaviest concentration of workers. Appendix table 21 shows this comparison. No significant differences were observed. The table supports the common-sense notion that this is an extremely homogeneous population. Accordingly, it was decided to select a sample only from the three postal zones in which there was the heaviest concentration of workers' residences.

The listing slips provided by Blue Cross for these three zones were shuffled and divided into packets of approximately twenty-five. By conventional random methods forty-five packets were selected of 1125 households.[2] The slips from which

2. Actually thirteen packets contained twenty-six slips so that the final sample consisted of 1,138 names and addresses.

the sample was selected were more than two years old. Sixty-two UAW workers included in the sample had moved out of the Maryland area or died. This left a total of 1,075 potential respondents. Of these, 937 were interviewed resulting in a completion rate of 87 percent. While the completion rate is conventionally considered suitable for population surveys of this type, it was higher than is necessary for analysis at the level of precision hoped for.

There were 139 refusals (13 percent of the potential respondents). Much effort was expended in attempting to "break" these refusals. For the entire sample a total of 2,942 "doorbell" calls were made by interviewers. The average number of calls for completed interviews was 2.2. For the "hard-core" refusal group, an average of 5.4 additional calls were made, as well as an untabulated number of phone calls. Budgetary limitations prevented further effort.

An enumeration giving age, sex, education, and relationship to the insured of each family member was obtained on sixty-four of these refusals. The age and education of those who would have been the respondent were compared to those of the respondents with completed interviews. There were significant differences. The average age of a respondent with a completed interview was 40.2 years. The average age of a refusal was 43.0. The average number of years of schooling of a respondent who completed an interview was 9.7 years, while those who refused to be interviewed averaged but 8.2 years. The greatest difference was found in average family size. The average family size of a respondent was 3.7; of a refusal, 2.1. The completed interviews underrepresent the older, less-educated workers living only with their spouse or another adult or else living alone.

Twenty interviews that were initially classed as repeated refusals were completed in whole or in part. These twenty interviews were compared to those that were not initial refusals. There were some differences in responses to the questions that are analyzed in this study. On the whole the group that refused to be interviewed admitted to less contact with the mentally ill and were more rejective of them. This fact should be borne in mind in generalizing the conclusions of the UAW study. Forty-nine completed interviews were eliminated from the tabulations presented in this report for a variety of reasons. Seven were with nonqualified respondents. In twelve cases the interviewers' reports indicated that the setting of the interview was such that some doubt existed as to the credibility of the responses. In twenty-eight cases the respondents, though administratively members of the insured group by Blue Cross regulation, were not actually members of the blue-collar working-class population reported on in this study. Two cases were lost through clerical error in the collating of the questionnaires that resulted in the omission of the social-distance questions.

In addition to the sample of UAW workers selected as described above, two other groups were interviewed with the same questionnaire. All patients in treatment at the Hopkins UAW Clinic at the time of the survey were interviewed. Under the terms of the prepayment plan that the United Automobile Workers had negotiated with General Motors, workers had the option of selecting their own physician or facility for care. However, to insure that the choice would not be necessarily restricted to psychiatrists engaged in private practice and lacking immediate access to inpatient and team resources, the Phipps Psychiatric Clinic of Hopkins Hospital organized such a comprehensive resource. This clinic is known as the UAW Clinic. Its patients are restricted to insured members of the UAW and their qualified dependents who seek psychiatric care. Through Blue Cross records of payment it was possible to determine the proportion of such care that was being rendered by the Hopkins UAW clinic. At the time of the survey the clinic was providing about 70 percent of all such care.

A second group interviewed in the same study were neighbors of the UAW respondents. In every fifteenth case the interviewer assignment called for an interview with an adult member of a randomly selected household in the same block as the respondent.[3] The completion rate for these respondents was 87 percent, not significantly different from that attained with the UAW respondents. The inclusion of these respondents allowed a comparison between UAW members and their immediate neighbors. Tabulations of these interviews with neighbors are not included in the general tabulations reported throughout the body of this work. The nature of the selection of these respondents limits their utility to that of a control group for the UAW respondents. Beyond that, they are not representative of any definable universe.

The sample as finally constituted consisted of a list of names and addresses. These were transcribed with an identification number on the questionnaires before distribution to the interviewer. The first step of the interview was an enumeration of all persons living in the dwelling unit, and their age, sex, and relationship to the person named on the questionnaire. Except for the neighbors this was always the name of the UAW member. In 50 percent of the cases where a spouse was living in the same dwelling unit, the spouse was the respondent. When no spouse was present the person whose name was written on the questionnaire was the respondent.

Unlike the Baltimore study, tabulations are reported on an unweighted sample. For purposes not connected with the data of this report, parallel tabulations have been computed with several different weightings. Marginal tabulations reported in this study do not differ in any instance from tabulations weighted by the number of adults in the household by a P of less than .30.

Interviewing for the study was done by a commercial research firm with twenty-five years of experience in the Baltimore area. The interviewers had an average of 6.2 years of experience in this type of work. Interviewers were given an intensive one-day training session on the particular questionnaire by

3. The addition or subtraction of a single-digit random number to or from the respondent's address determined these households.

the study director and an experienced field supervisor. The interviewers were told that they were conducting a study of health insurance, as indeed was the case. Since the attitudinal questions that are the subject of this report were only a small portion of the total questionnaire, there was no particular need to deemphasize them. They were the first part of the questionnaire to use the term "mental illness." Although the Hopkins sponsorship of the study could not be concealed from the interviewers, that of the Department of Psychiatry was. However, experienced interviewers tend to quickly conceptualize questionnaires and are normally inquisitive about the auspices under which they work. The detailed recordings required for a history of psychiatric illness could hardly be concealed, and many of their comments at the training session indicated an awareness that "psychiatric insurance" was the major focus of investigation. Throughout the period of the fieldwork the study director was not listed in the Hopkins directory. However, it would not have been difficult for an interviewer to identify his affiliation precisely.

As part of the study technique a debriefing session of the key interviewers was conducted at the conclusion of Wave II. At this session key tabulations were presented, and the interviewer's experience was explored for any factors that might have bearing on the meaning of the tabulations. When the tabulations of the social-distance and contact questions were presented, several interviewers expressed disbelief. They could recall nothing unusual in that particular aspect of the interview situation for either themselves or the respondents. It was simply the summary tabulations that surprised them.

Ten percent of all completed interviews were verified either by reinterview or by phone. No instance of interviewer "cheating" was discovered.

The Population Studied

How does this sample of UAW workers and their families compare with the total population living in the area and with their immediate neighbors? In the same area where the sampled UAW workers live there are 188,020 persons, according to the updated estimate based on the 1960 census. Of these, roughly 50 percent are male and 50 percent female. The same is not true of the UAW members or their neighbors. Among them males slightly outnumber females—52 percent to 48 percent. This may be due to the residential location within the census tracts of the population being studied. A majority of single men tend to live closest to the industrial manufacturing plants that employ predominantly male workers. Unattached males and male relatives might find it more convenient to reside in these particular areas. The same need not be true of female workers of the same skill level. There would be greater job opportunities for them in the various service industries.

Of all adults between the ages of twenty-one and sixty living in the same census tracts as the UAW respondents, the average age is 43.6; that of the UAW workers, 40.2 years; and that of neighbors, 45.4. When all members of a dwelling unit are considered, the average age of the UAW population remains younger than that of the total population, 23.6 as compared with 28.9. There is no age difference, however, between the UAW workers and their neighbors, both of whom average 23.3 years. The difference in the average ages of the UAW adults and the population is due to the larger number of elderly people living alone among the population. The UAW sample is by definition composed almost entirely of persons who are of working age.

There are significantly fewer adults who have never been married among the UAW population than there are among the total population of the census tracts (appendix table 22). Racially the populations are not very different. Among the total adult population of the area, 4 percent are black; among the sample of UAW workers, 3 percent.

In terms of education the union members do not differ significantly from those that live around them. The 106,000 adults in the area have attained an average of 9.6 years of education; the union members and their spouses, 9.7; their immediate neighbors, 9.8.

The greatest single difference between the UAW families and those that live around them is in terms of family income (appendix table 23). The sample of UAW families has a significantly higher annual family income than other families living in the same area.

The incomes reported for the population at large are those of 1960 while those for the UAW members are 1968. According to the Department of Labor, wages did rise during that period. Therefore, it is possible that the difference is not as great as reported. However, even the most extreme estimates of wage increases for the period under discussion—20 percent—would not result in the family income of the population at large approximating that of the UAW family. The sample of neighbors also reported family incomes substantially lower than that of their UAW neighbors.

Geographically and residentially this is quite a stable population. Fifty percent were born in the Baltimore area and still live there. Most of those who were born elsewhere and migrated did so before 1959. Sixty-four percent have lived at the same address for more than five years. This is also true of their immediate neighbors. Eighty-nine percent own their home, as do their neighbors.

Asked about religion, 51 percent designated themselves as Protestants, and 49 percent as Catholics. The average respondent reported "attending church services" twenty-two times in the past year. However, 25 percent reported attending only twice or less.

In terms of the Hollingshead Index of Social Position, all members of the sample are in the upper part of class IV (1957). Social class, but not income, is constant throughout the group. Typically, members live in their own two-story row house—a common architectural form in Baltimore. Homes are extremely similar in layout, room size, and basic equipment. Furnishings are of the mass-produced type purchased in department stores.

"Suites" of living room, dining room, and/or bedroom furniture are extremely frequent. Curtains, rugs, and/or carpeting are almost always present. Decorative objects are standardized and frequently of the "souvenir" type. No interviewer reported observing a single nonrepresentational picture. Books and magazines, however, were common. No home was without a television set, usually of the console type. As measured by interviewer judgment, furnishings and homes in more than 90 percent of the cases were clean and in good repair.

The average number of persons per dwelling unit was 3.7. This was slightly fewer than the 4.1 of their neighbors. Almost invariably a family consisted of parents and dependent children. Very few relatives or grandparents were enumerated, and only three boarders were recorded in the entire sample. For those who had dependent children there was an average of 1.6 children for each home.

In UAW families almost a quarter of the wives reported full-time employment, as did their neighbors. The most frequent occupations of the wives were sales clerks, clerical workers, and unskilled machine operators in that order.

The occupations reported for the UAW workers—all of whom were men—were those typical of an automobile assembly and finishing plant. In general the work requires a fair degree of skill and considerable reliability of performance and is moderately exacting in physical terms. Some jobs are extremely exacting physically and require the wearing of a respirator for most of the working day. Eighty-six percent reported themselves as generally satisfied with their job. The most frequent complaint was monotony and fatigue.

The effectiveness of the collective-bargaining process and solidarity of the union may be related to the high degree of job satisfaction. For example, shortly after the field survey, contract negotiations with General Motors broke down and a strike occurred. The strike vote in the local union being studied was virtually unanimous. The men maintained their strike in an orderly and disciplined manner with no coercion whatsoever and indeed remained on strike some days after the national settlement in order to reach agreement with management on several purely local issues.

The main paths of advancement for the UAW workers are through the accumulation of seniority and the benefits obtained by their union in labor-contract negotiations with General Motors. The average male UAW respondent had been employed in essentially the same job using essentially the same skills for 13.5 years. The same statistic for their neighbors was 7.5 years. The men advance as a group, rather than through the idealized American pattern of increasing education, skill, responsibility, and consequent increased compensation.

There is a considerable awareness of the social and economic aspects of unionism. For example, 54 percent of the men considered themselves "better off" than their fathers "as far as jobs" are concerned. When asked why, 86 percent answered in terms of the condition of their employment, specifically "wages," "hours," and "the union." In contrast less than half of their neighbors answered in the same manner.

As might be expected, formal education is not a particularly salient feature of the life experience of this population. Although over 90 percent reported that their fathers could read and write, fewer than half could even guess the number of years that their fathers had attended school. Of those that answered, the modal education of the parent reported was five to eight years.

The general attitudinal climate of the population is of particular interest in interpreting and generalizing answers to questions concerning the mentally ill and mental illnesses. Five statements from the "F" scale presumed to indicate authoritarianism had been included in the questionnaire (appendix table 24). As can be seen from the table, the two statements dealing with sexual matters are responded to in a liberal fashion by the overwhelming majority of respondents. However, the statements indicating an authoritarian bent were endorsed by substantial majorities.

Information was also obtained on voting behavior. The results are shown in appendix table 25. Fifty percent of the respondents had voted in the presidential election of 1964. Fifty-four percent voted in the 1968 election. Humphrey, the Democratic candidate, received almost 50 percent of the votes; Nixon, about 25 percent; and the independent segregationist Wallace, who appeared on the Maryland ballot, about 20 percent. The votes of the immediate neighbors of the UAW members were distributed in about the same proportions.

Forty-four percent gave party affiliation as the reason for their preference; 42 percent referred to the personal characteristics of the candidate, the "better man." These two reasons are not exclusive and many respondents gave both. Eighteen percent explained their preference in negative terms as the "lesser evil." Thirteen percent thought their candidate's stand on law and order was the most important reason for their vote while an equal number saw their candidate's "attitude toward labor" as significant. The same number mentioned "the war." Conspicuous by their absence were references to the issues of inflation, government spending, and taxes. In none of these reasons did the UAW members differ significantly from their immediate neighbors.

In summary, the social and political attitudes of the population surveyed do not appear unusually different from those of unionized working-class populations in general. They are neither extremely permissive nor "radical."

Sample for the Second Wave of Interviewing

Eighteen months after the initial survey, the same sample was resurveyed. In the interim there had been an educational campaign sponsored by the union and an increase in the number of patients at the clinic. The educational campaign consisted of: 1) monthly columns in the union newspaper on general mental health topics, with each column mentioning the availability of mental health care and reiterating the description of the psychiatric-insurance benefit; 2) attendance by the clinical director at several union meetings for brief addresses and question-answering by the clinic's personnel; 3) attendance at a shop stewards' meeting and a brief discussion of the clinic and psychiatric problems; and 4) the posting on the bulletin board of each plant of a card giving the name, address, and phone number of the clinic, and the name of the public health nurse attached to the clinic.

The main purpose of these activities was to inform the rank-and-file membership that their insurance benefits covered not only hospitalization, but also, without deduction, outpatient psychiatric care. This theme was reiterated in all talks and newspaper columns. It is doubtful if this campaign effectively reached more than a small fraction of the union membership. The initial survey had shown that only 26 percent of the respondents were aware that their insurance covered outpatient psychiatric care. On resurvey after the educational campaign, 33 percent were aware of this provision in their insurance benefit.

The initial population of the Wave II resurvey was the 888 respondents that had been interviewed in Wave I. Completed interviews were obtained in Wave II with 653 or 75 percent of the Wave I respondents. Of the original respondents, 235 were not interviewed. The reasons for these failures were as follows: moved, no forwarding address, no phone listing, etc, 34; deceased, hospitalized, too ill for interview, 12; could not find at home during field period, 37; refusals, 91; appointments for interview beyond limits of field period, 61.

The field budget for the second wave of the interviewing was stringently limited. The possibility of exhausting the budget before completing the field work was a realistic one in view of rising costs. Accordingly, the interviewers were not given their assignments in a conventional manner. One-half of the original respondents were randomly selected and assigned. These assignments were completely processed before the next interviewer assignments, one-half of the remainder, were randomly selected and distributed. Fieldwork was terminated after the final 222 respondents had been assigned.

Either all assigned respondents had been interviewed or at least two attempts were made to obtain an interview. The sixty-one cases listed as "appointments for interview beyond limits of field period" were respondents who had been contacted by either an interviewer in person or a field supervisor by phone and an appointment for an interview had been made at the earliest convenience of the respondent. Unfortunately, before these dates arrived, all fieldwork funds had been expended. The thirty-four respondents who had moved and had not been located had been checked through the post office and phone company. Additional funds for more complete checking through company records might well have reduced this number. The cases listed as deceased, hospitalized, or too ill for interview were definitely established to be so. Of those who were not at home during the period in which the study was in the field, some would undoubtedly have returned, and a more extended period of fieldwork might have reduced their number. All of these families were still at their present address. Phones had not been disconnected and furniture was in the home. In some instances the respondents had returned home for brief periods between attempts to contact them.

The refusal rate was only slightly in excess of 10 percent. There were individuals who had been contacted at least once by an interviewer and had refused to answer the questionnaire. Some had been contacted twice and continued to maintain their refusal. The most frequent ground for refusal was that they had already answered the questionnaire. As a result of the verification procedure, some had indeed answered the questionnaire twice.

It required an average of 2.0 calls to complete an interview in Wave II as compared with 2.2 in Wave I. More than 260 phone calls were made to obtain the interviews. These do not include calls made for the location of respondents who had moved. Among those interviewed 9 percent had changed their address from the time of the previous interview. No verification procedure was employed or required in Wave II interviewing. Most of the interviewers had not been employed in the first wave. Demographic data available on individual respondents obtained in the first wave could be compared directly with the same data in the second wave. Such comparisons were made, and no unexplainable discrepancies were discovered.

The completed interviews of Wave II were compared with the original 888 obtained on Wave I. The purpose of the comparison was to test the possibility that the interviewing failures of Wave II were concentrated in some particular category. The percentage of loss was approximately the same for both sexes, both races, all age groups, income levels, educational levels, and family size. Nevertheless, the fact still remains that the completed interviews were those that were easiest to obtain, while the uninterviewed for whatever reason were those that were the more difficult.

In addition to the sample described above, thirty-three patients in active treatment at the UAW Clinic at the time of the survey were also interviewed. Unless specifically noted, they are not included in the tabulations presented in this work.

Bibliography

Ackerknecht, E. H. 1942a. "Primitive Medicine and Culture Pattern." *Bulletin of Historical Medicine* 12:545-74.

______. 1942b. "Psychopathology, Primitive Medicine and Primitive Culture." *Bulletin of Historical Medicine* 14:30.

Ackerman, N. W. 1965. "The Social Psychology of Prejudice." *Mental Hygiene* 49:27-35.

Adland, B. 1937. *Attitudes of Eastern European Jews Toward Mental Illness.* Smith College Studies in Social Work, vol. 8.

Adorno, T. W.; Frenkel-Brunswick, E.; Levinson, D. J.; and Newitt-Sanford, R. 1950. *The Authoritarian Personality.* New York: Harper and Row.

Alexander, F. G., and Selesnick, S. T. 1966. *The History of Psychiatry.* New York: Harper and Row.

Allen, L. 1943. "Study of Community Attitudes Toward Mental Hygiene." *Mental Hygiene* 27:248-54.

Allport, G. W. 1951. "Prejudice, a Problem in Psychological and Social Causation." In *Toward a General Theory of Action.* Cambridge: Harvard University Press.

______. 1954. *The Nature of Prejudice.* Garden City, N.Y.: Doubleday.

Altrocchi, J., and Eisdorfer, C. 1961. "Changes in Attitudes Towards Mental Illness." *Mental Illness* 45:563-70.

Audience Research, Inc. 1954a. *New Jersey Mental Health Survey of General Public.* Princeton, N.J.

______. 1954b. *New Jersey Mental Health Survey of Physicians.* Princeton, N.J.

Beers, C. W. 1908. *A Mind That Found Itself.* New York: Doubleday.

Becker, Howard S. 1963. *Outsiders.* Glencoe, Ill.: Free Press.

Bell, N. 1953. "Family Reactions to Strain." Master's thesis, University of Toronto.

Belson, W. 1957. "The Ideas of the Television Public About Mental Illness." *Mental Health* 16:95.

Bettelheim, B., and Janowitz, M. 1950. *Dynamics of Prejudice: A Psychological and Sociological Study of Veterans.* New York: Harper and Row.

Bingham, J. 1951. "What the Public Thinks of Psychiatry." *American Journal of Psychiatry* 107:599-601.

Biographical Directory of the Fellows and Members of the American Psychiatric Association. 1968. Published for the American Psychiatric Association. New York: Bowker.

Bogardus, E. S. 1925. "Measuring Social Distance." *Journal of Applied Sociology* 9:299-308.

______. 1928. *Immigration and Race Attitudes.* Boston: D. C. Heath.

Brown, R. 1965. *Social Psychology.* New York: Free Press.

Cattell, R. D. 1948. "Ethics and Social Sciences." *American Psychologist* 3:195.

Chin-Shong, E. 1968. "Rejection of the Mentally Ill: A Comparison with the Findings of Ethnic Prejudice." Ph.D. dissertation, Columbia University.

Clausen, J. A., and Yarrow, Marian R. 1955. "The Impact of Mental Illness on the Family." *Journal of Social Issues* 11:1-64.

______. 1959. "The Sociology of Mental Illness." In *Sociology Today,* ed. R. K. Merton, L. Broom, and L. S. Cottrell, pp. 485-508. New York: Basic Books.

______. 1963. "Sociology of Mental Disease." In *Handbook of Medical Sociology,* ed. Freeman, Lotise, and Reeder. Englewood Cliffs, N.J.: Prentice-Hall.

______. 1966. "Mental Disorders." In *Contemporary Social Problems,* ed. R. K. Merton, and R. A. Nisbet, pp. 26-83. New York: Harcourt, Brace & World.

Cohen, Albert K. 1959. "The Study of Social Disorganization & Deviant Behavior." In *Sociology Today,* ed. R. K. Merton, L. Broom, and L. S. Cottrell, pp. 461-84. New York: Basic Books.

Couch, A., and Kenniston, K. 1960. "Yea Sayers and Nay Sayers: Agreeing Response Set as a Personality Variable." *Journal of Abnormal Social Psychology* 60:151-74.

Crawford, F., and Rollins, G. 1960. "Discharged Patients: Liability or Asset." Paper given at the Institute on Changing Concepts in Hospitalization Rehabilitation, September 1960.

Crawford, F. R.; Rollins, G. W.; and Sutherland, R. L. 1960. "Variations Between Negros and Whites in Concepts of Mental Illness and Its Treatment." *Annals of the New York Academy of Science* 84:918-37.

Crocetti, Guido M. 1955. "Study of Patient Stay, Movement and Disposition in City Psychiatric Hospitals." New York.

Crocetti, G. M., and Lemkau, P. V. 1963. "Public Opinion of Psychiatric Home Care in an Urban Area." *American Journal of Public Health* 53:409–14.

Crutcher, H. B. 1944. *Foster Home Care for Mental Patients.* New York: Commonwealth Fund.

Cumming, E., and Cumming, J. 1957. *Closed Ranks.* Cambridge, Mass.: Harvard University Press.

______. 1959. "Relatives' Attitudes and Mental Hospitalization." *Mental Hygiene,* 43, no. 2 (April, 1959).

______. 1965. "On the Stigma of Mental Illness." *Community Mental Health Journal* 1:135–43.

Davis, K. 1938. "Mental Hygiene and the Class Structure." *Psychiatry* 1:55–65.

Deutsch, A. 1948. *The Shame of the States.* New York: Harcourt.

______. 1949. *The Mentally Ill in America.* 2d. ed. New York: Columbia University Press.

Dickman, H. R., and McKenzie, R. A. 1960. "Attitudes of High School Students Toward Institutions, Illness, and Treatment." VA Hospital, Roseburg, Ore., January 1960.

Dohrenwend, B. P. 1966. "Social Status and Psychological Disorder: An Issue of Substance and an Issue of Method." *American Sociological Review* 31:14–34.

Dohrenwend, B. P.; Bernard, V. W.; and Kolb, L. C. 1962. "The Orientations of Leaders in an Urban Area Toward Problems of Mental Illness." *American Journal of Psychiatry* 118:683-91.

Dohrenwend, B. P., and Chin-Shong, E. 1967. "Social Status and Attitudes Towards Psychological Disorder: The Problem of Tolerance of Deviance." *American Sociological Review* 32:417–33.

Dohrenwend, B. P., and Crandell, D. 1967. "Some Relations Among Psychiatric Symptoms, Organic Illness and Social Class." *American Journal of Psychiatry* 123:1527–38.

Dollard, J. 1934. "The Psychotic Person Seen Culturally." *American Journal of Sociology* 39:637–48.

Durkheim, E. 1947. *The Division of Labor in Society.* Glencoe, Ill.: Free Press.

______. 1950. *The Rules of Sociological Method.* 8th ed. Glencoe, Ill.: Free Press.

Eaton, J. W., and Weil, R. G. 1955. *Culture and Mental Disorders.* Glencoe, Ill.: Free Press.

Edgerton, W. J., and Bentz, W. K. 1969. "Attitudes and Opinions of Rural People About Mental Illness and Program Services." *American Journal of Public Health* 59:470–77.

Elinson, J.; Padilla, E.; and Perkins, M. 1967. *Public Image of Mental*

Health Services. New York: Mental Health Materials Center.

Ellenberger, H. S. 1970. *The Discovery of the Unconscious*. New York: Basic Books.

Erickson, K. T. 1962. "Data on the Sociology of Deviance." *Social Problems* 9:308.

Faris, R., and Dunham, W. 1939. *Mental Disorders in Urban Areas*. Chicago: University of Chicago Press.

Felix, R. H. et al. 1959. *Social Psychiatry and Community Attitudes*. World Health Organization Technical Report Series no. 177. Geneva: World Health Organization.

______. 1967. *Mental Illness: Progress and Prospects*. New York: Columbia University Press.

Freeman, H. E. 1961. "Attitudes Toward Mental Illness Among Relatives of Former Patients." *American Sociological Review* 26:59–66.

Freeman, H. E., and Kassebaum, G. G. 1960. "The Relationship of Education and Knowledge to Opinions About Mental Illness." *Mental Hygiene* 44:43–47.

Freeman, H. E., and Simmons, O. G. 1961a. "Feelings of Stigma Among Relatives of Former Mental Patients." *Social Problems* 8:312–21.

______. 1961b. "Treatment Experiences of Mental Patients and Their Families." *American Journal of Public Health and the Nation's Health* 51:1266–73.

______. 1963. *The Mental Patient Comes Home*. New York: John Wiley & Sons.

Friedman, T. T.; Rolfe, P.; and Perry, S. "Home Treatment of Psychiatric Patients." *The American Journal of Psychiatry* 116:807–09.

Gelfand, S., and Ullman, L. P. 1961. "Change in Attitudes About Mental Illness Associated With Clerkship Training." *The International Journal of Social Psychiatry*, 7, no. 4:292–98.

Gerbner, G. 1961. "Psychology, Psychiatry and Mental Illness in the Mass Media: A Study of Trends." *Mental Hygiene* 45:89–93.

Gibbs, J. P. 1962. "Rates of Mental Hospitalization: A Study of Social Reaction to Deviant Behavior." *American Sociological Review*, 27, no. 6 (December 1962).

Goffman, E. 1963. *Stigma; Notes on the Management of Spoiled Identity*. Englewood Cliffs, N.J.: Prentice-Hall.

Gordon, Gerald A. 1966. *Role Theory and Illness: A Sociological Perspective*. New Haven, Conn.: College and University Press.

Gould, J., and Kolb, W. L. 1964. *A Dictionary of the Social Sciences*. New York: Free Press.

Grad, J., and Sainsbury, P. 1966. "Problems of Caring for the Mentally Ill at Home." *Proceedings of the Royal Society of Medicine* 59:20-23.

______. 1963. "Mental Illness and the Family." *Lancet* 1:544-47.

Grad, J.; Sainsbury, P.; and Collins, J. 1962. "Home Care for the Mentally Ill: Its Effect on the Family." Paper presented to the International Congress of Sociology, Washington, D.C., September 1962.

Gruenberg, E. M., and Bellin, S. S. 1957. "The Impact of Mental Disease on Society." In *Explorations in Social Psychiatry*, ed. A. H. Leighton, J. A. Clausen, and R. N. Wilson, pp. 341-64. New York: Basic Books.

Gurin, G.; Veroff, V.; and Feld, S. 1960. *Americans View Their Mental Health: A Nationwide Interview Survey.* New York: Basic Books.

Halpert, H. P. 1969. "Public Acceptance of the Mentally Ill: An Exploration of Attitudes." *Public Health Report* 84:59-64.

Harding, J.; Jutner, B.; Proshansky, H.; and Chein, I. 1964. "Prejudice and Ethnic Relations." In *Handbook of Social Psychology*, ed. G. Lindzey, vol. 3, pp. 1021-61. Cambridge, Mass.: Addison-Wesley.

Harman, H. 1960. *Modern Factor Analysis.* Chicago: University of Chicago Press.

Hollingshead, August B. 1957. "Two-Factor Index of Social Position." New Haven: 1965 Yale Station. Mimeographed.

Hollingshead, A. B. and Redlich, F. C. 1958. *Social Class and Mental Illness.* New York: Wiley.

Hospital Council of Greater New York. 1956. *Organized Home Medical Care in New York City: A Study of Nineteen Programs*, Peter Rogatz, and Guido M. Crocetti. Cambridge, Mass.: Harvard University Press.

Hotelling, H. 1936. "Relations Between Two Sets of Variates." *Biom* 28:321-27.

Hunt, R. C. 1958. "Ingredients of a Rehabilitation Program: An Approach to the Prevention of Disability from Chronic Psychoses." *Proceedings of the 34th Annual Conference of the Milbank Memorial Fund*, 1957, part I.

Hyman, H., and Sheatsley, P. 1954. *Interviewing for Social Research.* Chicago: University of Chicago Press.

Jaco, E. G. 1957a. "Attitudes Towards and Incidence of Mental Disorders: A Research Note." *Southwestern Social Science Quarterly* 38:27-38.

______. 1957b. "Social Factors in Mental Disorders in Texas." *Social Problems* 4:322-28.

———. 1960. *The Social Epidemiology of Mental Disorders.* New York: Russell Sage Foundation.

Jahoda, M. 1955. "Toward a Social Psychology of Mental Health." In *Mental Health and Mental Disorder,* ed. Arnold M. Rose. New York: Norton.

Joint Commission on Mental Illness and Health. 1961. *Action for Mental Health.* Final report. New York: Basic Books.

Kadushin, A. 1957. "Opposition to Referral for Psychiatric Treatment." *Social Work* 14:81-83.

Kadushin, C. 1964. "Social Class and the Experience of Ill Health." *Sociological Inquiry* 24:67-80.

Kentucky Mental Health Planning Commission. 1964. *Kentuckians' Attitudes Toward Mental Illness.* Louisville, Ky.

Kepner, C., and Fortier, J. 1954. "The Melville Project." A study of Community Education, September 1952. Saskatchewan Division of Canadian Mental Health Association, July 6–September 17, 1954.

Kepner, C.; Kepner, L.; and Dixon, A. 1954. "The Rehabilitation of Mental Patients." A study conducted for the Saskatchewan Division of the Canadian Mental Health Association, July 6–September 17, 1954, in Regina, Saskatchewan.

Kharma, J. L.; Pratt, S.; and Gardiner, G. A. 1960. "Attitudes Toward Criminally Insane Patients." Larned State Hospital, Kansas.

Knight, O. B. 1968. "Decrease in Social Distance as a Consequence of Interaction: A Pilot Study." *California Journal of Educational Research* 19:121.

Kraepelin, E. 1919. *Dementia Praecox.* Edinburgh: E. & S. Livingstone, Ltd.

Kramer, R. J. 1956. "A Measure of Community Attitudes Toward Mental Illness." Masters thesis, University of Michigan.

Krech, N., and Crutchfield, R. S. 1948. *Theory and Problems of Social Psychology.* New York: McGraw-Hill.

Landy, D., and Griffith, W. D. 1958. "Employer Receptivity Toward Hiring Psychiatric Patients." *Mental Hygiene* 42:383-90.

Lawrence, P. S. 1958. "Chronic Illness and Socio-Economic Status." In *Patients, Physicians and Illness,* ed. E. Garthy Jaco, pp. 37-49. Glencoe, Ill.: Free Press.

Lemkau, M. 1962. "Professional and Public Attitudes Regarding the Care of Mental Patients in Carroll County, Maryland." Senior Honors Thesis in Sociology at Western Maryland College. Mimeographed.

Lemkau, P. V. 1965. "An Evaluation of Evidence Suggesting Improvement in Attitudes Toward the Mentally Ill." Paper presented to the Annual Convention of the American Psychological Association, September 4, 1965.

Lemkau, P. V., and Crocetti, G. M. 1961. "The Amsterdam Municipal Psychiatric Service: A Psychiatric-Sociologic Review." *American Journal of Psychiatry,* 117, no. 9 (March 1961).

_____. 1962. "An Urban Population's Opinions and Knowledge About Mental Illness." *American Journal of Psychiatry* 118:692-700.

_____. 1963. See Crocetti, G. M., and Lemkau, P. V.

Lippman, W. 1922. *Public Opinion, New York.* New York: Harcourt Brace.

MacLean, U. 1969. "Community Attitudes to Mental Illness in Edinburgh." *British Journal of Preventive and Social Medicine* 23:45-52.

MacMillan, Allistair M. 1957. "The Health Opinion Survey: Technique for Estimating Prevalence of Psychoneurotic and Related Types of Disorder in Communities." *Psychological Reports* 1:325-39.

Malsberg, B. 1944. *Mental Disease Among American Negroes: A Statistical Analysis, Characteristic of the American Negro.* New York: Harper.

Margolin, R. J. 1961. "A Survey of Employer Reactions to Known Former Mental Patients Working in Their Firms." *Mental Hygiene* 45:110-15.

Meldman, M. J. 1970. *Diseases of Attention and Perception.* New York: Pergamon.

Merton, R. K. 1957. *Social Theory and Social Structure.* Glencoe, Ill.: Free Press.

Merton, R. K.; Broom, L.; and Cottrell, L. S., eds. 1959. *Sociology Today.* New York: Basic Books.

Meyer, J. K. 1964. "Attitudes Toward Mental Illness in a Maryland Community." *Public Health Report* 79:769-72.

Michael, S. T. 1960. "Social Attitudes, Socio-Economic Status & Psychiatric Symptoms." *Acta Psychiatrica Ft. Neurologica Scandinavica,* 35, fasc. 4.

Miller, M., and Mishler, E. G. 1959. "Social Class, Mental Illness and American Psychiatry." *Milbank Memorial Fund Quarterly* 37:174-79.

Mills, C. W. 1943. "The Professional Ideology of Social Pathologists." *American Journal of Sociology* 49:165-80.

Mulfad, C. L. 1968. "Ethnocentrism and Attitudes Towards the

Mentally Ill." *Sociology Quarterly* 9:107.
Murdock, G. P. 1949. *Social Structure.* New York: Macmillan Co.
Murphy, G.; Murphy, L. B.; and Newcomb, T. M. 1937. *Experimental Social Psychology: An Interpretation of Research Upon the Socialization of the Individual.* New York: Harper & Brothers.
Nudelman, A. E. 1965. "Temperamental Conservatism, Authoritarianism and Rejection of the Mentally Ill and Psychiatry." *Mental Hygiene* 49:493.
Nunnally, J. C., Jr. 1961. *Popular Conceptions of Mental Health, Their Development and Change.* New York: Holt, Rinehart and Winston.
Olshansky, S.; Grob, S.; and Malamud, I. 1958. "Employer Attitudes and Practices in the Hiring of Ex-Mental Patients." *Mental Hygiene* 42:399-401.
Parrington, V. L. 1930. *Main Currents in American Thought: An Interpretation of American Literature from the Beginnings to 1920.* New York: Harcourt, Brace, and Co.
Parsons, T. 1958. "Definitions of Health and Illness in the Light of American Values and Social Structure." In *Patients, Physicians and Illness,* ed. E. C. Jaco, pp. 165-87. Glencoe, Ill.: Free Press.
Parsons, T., and Fox, R. 1952. "Illness Therapy and the Modern Urban Family." *Journal of Social Issues* 8:31-44.
Pearse, I. H., and Crocker, L. H. 1943. *The Peckham Experiment.* London: Allen and Unwin.
Phillips, D. L. 1963. "A Possible Consequence of Seeking Help for Mental Disorder." *American Sociological Review* 18:963-72.
———. 1964. "Rejection of the Mentally Ill." *American Sociological Review* 19:679-87.
———. 1967. "Education, Psychiatric Sophistication and the Rejection of Mentally Ill Help-Seekers." *Sociology Quarterly* 8:122.
Pollock, H. M. 1945. "A Brief History of Family Care of Mental Patients in America." *American Journal of Psychiatry* 102:351-61.
Pratt, S.; Giannitrapani, D.; and Khanna, P. 1960. "Attitudes Toward the Mental Hospital and Selected Population Characteristics." *Journal of Clinical Psychology* 16:241-48.
Purdue University. 1959. "Youth's Attitudes Toward Mental Illness." Purdue Opinion Panel, Report of Poll #56. Lafayette, Ind.: Purdue University, Division of Educational Referents.
Ramsey, G. V., and Siepp, M. 1948. "Attitudes and Opinions Concerning Mental Illness." *Psychiatric Quarterly* 22:428-44.
Ridenour, N. 1961. *Mental Health in the United States; A Fifty-Year History.* Cambridge: Harvard University Press.

Rootman, A., and Lafare, P. 1965. "Ethnic Community." *Psychiatric Quarterly* 41:211-21.

Roper, Elmo, & Assoc. "People's Attitudes Concerning Mental Health: A Study Made in the City of Louisville." For the City of Louisville and *Colliers Magazine,* Copy No. 78, p. 45. Mimeographed.

Rose, C. L. 1959. "Relatives' Attitudes and Mental Hospitalization." *Mental Hygiene* 43:194-203.

Rosen, G. 1958. *A History of Public Health.* New York: M. D. Publications.

Sarbin, T. R., and Mancuso, J. D. 1970. "Failure of a Moral Enterprise: Attitudes of the Public Toward Mental Illness." *Journal of Consulting Psychology,* 35, no. 2:157-73.

Scheff, T. J. 1963. "Social Support for Stereotypes of Mental Disorder." *Mental Hygiene* 47:461-69.

______. 1966. *Being Mentally Ill: A Sociological Theory.* Chicago: Aldini Publishing Co.

______. 1970. "Schizophrenia as Ideology." *Schizophrenia Bulletin* 2:15-19. Schwartz, C. G. 1953. *Analysis of the Literature on the Rehabilitation of Mental Hospital Patients.* Washington, D.C.: National Institute of Mental Health.

______. 1952. *The Rehabilitation of Mental Hospital Patients.* Washington, D.C.: National Institute of Mental Health.

______. 1956. "The Stigma of Mental Illness." *Journal of Rehabilitation* 4:7-10.

______. 1957. "Perspectives of Deviance—Wives' Definitions of Their Husbands' Mental Illness." *Psychiatry* 20:275-91.

Sherman, H. 1962. "The Knowledge & Attitudes of the Senior Class of a Florida High School, 1960-1961, Toward the Leon County Mental Health Clinic." Tallahassee, Fla. Abstract of Paper.

Siassi, I.; Crocetti, G. M.; Spiro, H. R. 1973. "Feelings of Alienation in a Blue Collar Population." *Archives of General Psychiatry.*

Sigerist, H. E. 1951. *A History of Medicine,* vol. I. New York: Oxford University Press.

Silverman, I. G. 1967. "Sociology and Psychiatry." In *A Comprehensive Textbook of Psychiatry,* ed. Alfred M. Freedman and Harold I. Kaplan. Baltimore: Williams & Wilkins.

Somer, R., and Hall, R. 1958. "Alienation & Mental Illness." *American Sociological Review* 23:418.

Spiro, H. R. 1968. "Chronic Factitious Illness." *Archives of General Psychiatry* 18:569-79.

Spiro, H. R.; Siassi, I.; and Crocetti, G. M. 1972. "What Gets Surveyed in a Psychiatric Survey? A Case Study of the MacMillan Index."

Journal of Nervous and Mental Disease 154:105–14.

Stanton, A. H., and Schwartz, M. S. 1954. *The Mental Hospital.* New York: Basic Books.

Star, S. A. 1952. "Confidential Forecast of the Results of the Survey: Popular Thinking in the Field of Mental Health." National Opinion Research Center, University of Chicago, Survey no. 272, September 1952.

______. 1952. "What the Public Thinks About Mental Health and Mental Illness." Paper presented at the Annual Meeting of the National Association for Mental Health, Inc., November 19, 1952.

______. 1955a. "Public Attitudes: A Measure of the Difficulties." *Psychiatry, the Press and the Public.* June 1955.

______. "The Public's Ideas About Mental Illness." 1955b. National Opinion Research Center, University of Chicago.

______. 1955c. Speech given at the National Association for Mental Health. AAPOR 5/9/57.

______. 1957. "The Place of Psychiatry in Popular Thinking." Paper presented at the annual Association for the Advancement of Public Opinion Research meeting, Shoreham Hotel, Washington, D.C.

Stewart, D. D. 1955. "Posthospital Social Adjustment of Former Mental Patients From Two Arkansas Counties." *Southwestern Social Science Quarterly* 35:319.

Sullivan, H. S. 1956. *Clinical Studies in Psychiatry,* ed. H. S. Perry, M. L. Gawel, and M. Gibbon. New York: Norton.

Szasz, T. S. 1961. *The Myth of Mental Illness; Foundations of a Theory of Personal Conduct.* New York: Hoeber-Harper.

U.S. Bureau of the Census. 1960. *U.S. Census Characteristics of the Population.* Washington, D.C.: Government Printing Office.

Warner, J. 1937. "The Society, the Individual, and His Mental Disorders." *American Journal of Psychology,* September 1937.

Whatley, C. 1959. "Social Attitudes Towards Discharged Mental Patients." *Social Problems* 6:313–20.

______. 1963. "Status, Role and Vocational Continuity of Discharged Mental Patients." *Journal of Health and Human Behavior,* no. 4:105–12.

______. 1964. "Employer Attitudes, Discharged Patients, and Job Durability." *Mental Hygiene* 48:121–31.

Williams, J. H.; Williams, H. M.; Gavin, J.; and Grigg, C. M. 1962. "Attitudes Towards the Mentally Ill of a Sample of College Students and Professional Nurses." Institute for Social Research, Florida State University, Tallahassee, Fla., no. 5, June 1962.

Winnicott, D. C. 1949. "Hate and Countertransference." *International Journal of Psychoanalysis,* vol. 30, pt. 2.

Woodward, J. L. 1951. "Changing Ideas of Mental Illness and Its Treatment." *American Sociological Review* 16:443–54.

Wright, F. H. 1960. "Public Attitudes Toward Mental Illness in Various Locations in the United States and Britain." Personal communication.

Yarrow, M. R.; Clausen, J. A.; and Robbins, P. R. 1955. "The Social Meaning of Mental Illness." *Journal of Social Issues,* 11, no. 4:33–48.

Index

Titles in the Series

ANATOMY OF A COORDINATING COUNCIL
Implications for Planning
Basil J. F. Mott

BRITISH PRIVATE MEDICAL PRACTICE AND THE NATIONAL HEALTH SERVICE
Samuel Mencher

CHILD CARE WORK WITH EMOTIONALLY DISTURBED CHILDREN
Genevieve W. Foster, Karen Dahlberg VanderVen et al.

CHILDREN IN JEOPARDY
A Study of Abused Minors and Their Families
Elizabeth Elmer

CONTEMPORARY ATTITUDES TOWARD MENTAL ILLNESS
Guido M. Crocetti, Herzl R. Spiro, and Iradj Siassi

DENTISTS, PATIENTS, AND AUXILIARIES
Margaret Cussler and Evelyn W. Gordon

DYNAMICS OF INSTITUTIONAL CHANGE
The Hospital in Transition
Milton Greenblatt, Myron R. Sharaf, and Evelyn M. Stone

EDUCATION AND MANPOWER FOR COMMUNITY HEALTH
Hilary G. Fry, with William P. Shepard and Ray H. Elling

A GUIDE TO MENTAL HEALTH SERVICES
Edward T. Heck, Angel G. Gomez, and George L. Adams

HANDICAP
A Study of Physically Handicapped Children and Their Families
Joan K. McMichael

HOME TREATMENT
Spearhead of Community Psychiatry
Leonard Weiner, Alvin Becker, and Tobias T. Friedman

LONG-TERM CHILDHOOD ILLNESS
Harry A. Sultz, Edward R. Schlesinger, William E. Mosher, and Joseph G. Feldman

MARRIAGE AND MENTAL HANDICAP
Janet Mattinson

METHODOLOGY IN EVALUATING THE QUALITY OF MEDICAL CARE
An Annotated Selected Bibliography, 1955–1968
Isidore Altman, Alice J. Anderson, and Kathleen Barker

MIGRANTS AND MALARIA IN AFRICA
R. Mansell Prothero

A PSYCHIATRIC RECORD MANUAL FOR THE HOSPITAL
Dorothy Smith Keller

RACISM AND MENTAL HEALTH
Charles V. Willie, Bernard M. Kramer, and Bertram S. Brown, Editors